MW01633787

ATTACK THE
LUSITANIA!

ATTACK THE LUSITANIA!

A WORLD WAR I NOVEL

JERRY BORROWMAN

Covenant Communications, Inc.

Cover imageSink on Sight, The Story of the Submarine, 1981 (gouache on paper) by Mike Tregenza (Michael) (20th Century) Private Collection/ © Look and Learn/ The Bridgeman Art Library
Nationality / copyright status: English / out of copyright

Published by Covenant Communications, Inc.
American Fork, Utah

This is a work of fiction. The characters, names, incidents, places, and dialogue are either products of the author's imagination, and are not to be construed as real, or are used fictitiously.

Printed in the United States of America
First Printing: April 2011

17 16 15 14 13 12 11 10 9 8 7 6 5 4 3 2 1

ISBN 978-1-60861-223-9

To my friends and associates at Covenant Communications, Inc. I wish I could name each individually since they have become such an important part of my life in the past two decades. From cover design to distribution, editorial to publicity, administration and accounting—it is because of them that so many great books from so many outstanding authors find their way to you. I'm glad to be part of their family.

Acknowledgments

I'd like to thank a number of readers who helped with this book, including my wife, Marcella, who always does a great job checking the story for consistency and authenticity. I also appreciate the feedback provided by Shaun Pace, Norman Jenson, Wayne Borrowman, and Evan Rowley. Special love to Maya and Aaron Borrowman. I particularly value the contribution of Kirk Shaw, my editor at Covenant Communications, for his insight and encouragement. I have come to trust Kirk's judgment and editorial insight and consider him my friend and confidant.

Chapter 1
"Gott Strafe England"

March 1915—Irish Channel near Liverpool, England

"Increase revolutions to full speed."

"Aye, Captain." First Officer Braun repeated the order into the voice tube, and the vibration of the ship increased noticeably as the powerful German-built Korting diesel engines responded to the increased demand.

Captain Johann Weisig, captain of the U-boat, leaned into the metal coving that surrounded the bridge of his submarine. It had been a frustrating voyage, with raging storms leaving his crew of thirty-two sick and demoralized; two torpedoes having malfunctioned, allowing his prey to escape unharmed; and the only other viable target proving too fast for them to get a good clean shot. Now fuel was running low and they had a belly full of unused torpedoes—a disgrace that would be hard to explain when they returned to their base in Heligoland, Germany. He pounded his fist on the metal guard rail and cursed.

"Problem, sir?"

Weisig turned to Braun. "I can't believe there are no ships. This is the busiest port in Western England—where are the ships? We need targets." It was unusual for frustration to betray Weisig's normally cool demeanor.

"Military targets are few and far between . . ." Before Braun could finish his sentence, Weisig turned on him sharply.

"We've had this discussion before! All ships are military targets—there is no such thing as civilian or neutral ships since England imposed their blockade. I will not discuss this again."

"My apologies. It was just a lapse to earlier protocols." Braun certainly knew his place, and it was not to criticize the captain.

Weisig pumped his fist more lightly on the railing. "The English are so smug in their self-righteousness—we are condemned by the world for declaring unrestricted warfare on civilian and military targets, yet they are starving hundreds of thousands of women and children in Germany. Why should we sit idly by as America ships vast quantities of food and war supplies to English ports while denying sustenance to Germany? Neutral indeed! Are German civilian lives worth any less than English or American? Is death by hunger less painful than death by torpedo? What other possible response can there be than the one we have chosen?"

"None, of course; the old rules are obsolete in a modern war." In spite of Weisig's protests, Braun knew that the thought of firing on neutrals and innocents was repugnant to his captain. Weisig could pound his fist if he wanted, but Braun was there when Weisig expressed his astonishment and contempt that the captain of *U-20,* Walther Schweiger, had fired a torpedo at a hospital ship just a month earlier. The torpedo missed, but the protests around the world were ferocious, while Schweiger justified it as firing on enemy combatants. Unless his captain's views had changed dramatically since then, Weisig was still struggling with Germany's new policy of unrestricted warfare.

Braun hoped that Weisig was through discussing it, but he apparently wasn't. "They expect us to surface when we plan to launch an attack, fire a warning shot across the bow, and then give the crew and passengers time to leisurely make their way to lifeboats while we float naked and exposed as their destroyers swoop down to destroy us. It is madness."

"Yes, sir."

Weisig straightened up, as if he realized that he had revealed too much emotion. Above all else, a ship's captain was expected to be unflappable, even when the ship was nothing more than a submersible boat with a crew of just thirty-plus men. "Well, enough of that—call me if you see anything that floats. Its origins and cargo are no concern of mine."

"Sir!" Braun snapped to attention as Weisig descended the ladder in the conning tower that took him deep into the bowels of the small but savagely effective U-boat.

He made his way to his bunk and lay down for a much-overdue rest. His eyelids were just starting to relax when the intercom buzzed.

"Captain to the bridge!"

Weisig was out of his bunk and up the ladder in less time than it would take a cat to attack and kill a bird.

"What is it?"

"Off port side . . . there!" Weisig followed Braun's pointing finger to the edge of the horizon where he saw what looked like a smudge on a pair of glasses. "The lookout reported it just thirty seconds ago. You were summoned immediately."

Weisig strained through his powerful Zeiss binoculars. "I've got it! All hands to battle stations. Prepare to dive!"

"All hands to battle stations!" Braun repeated firmly as he pushed the alarm. The German equivalent of a Klaxon horn sounded throughout the ship, and a flurry of activity ensued as the lookouts secured their place at the top of the conning tower and then slid down to the platform. Weisig was already below by the time Braun took one last look at the object—quite clearly now a coal-fired ship lumbering heavily through the dark waters of the Irish Sea.

"Gott strafe England!" someone shouted. It was a popular new song in Germany that translated as "God punish England." Many called it the hate song. It was a hard sentiment for Braun to accept. Like many Germans before him, he had spent a number of years living in London. Even the royal family of England was of German descent, with Germany's Kaiser Wilhelm of the House of Hohenzollern a cousin to England's King Edward. Braun despised the fact that two countries with such a powerful shared heritage should be at war with each other. "Was it not the Prussian Prince Blücher who helped the English defeat Napoleon at Waterloo?" Now it was England and France who were allies, doing their best to strangle the very lifeblood out of the German state. "God punish England," Braun repeated in English. "And," thinking of his conversation with Weisig, "I suppose that it is we in this boat who are to be the instrument of that punishment." He quickly descended enough steps of the ladder to reach up and pull the hatch behind him, quickly turning the wheel to make it watertight. He descended the rest of the way into the belly of the beast.

"Take a look, Mr. Braun." The captain stepped back from the periscope.

Braun stepped forward, removed his eyeglasses, and peered into the narrow lenses of the periscope. It was difficult enough to make things out in broad daylight, but in the dusk it all appeared gray to him. Telling himself to concentrate, he narrowed his eyes to sharpen their focus. Finally he saw a ship come into view. "A freighter," he said evenly, greatly relieved that it was not a passenger ship.

"Nationality?"

He strained even harder, and then his eyes widened. "American!"

He pulled away from the periscope and turned to the captain, who said, "That's what I thought. I suspect we'll be on the front page of the *New York Times* tomorrow."

"There will be a firestorm of criticism, that's for sure."

Weisig stepped forward as Braun slipped quickly out of the way. It was time for a firing solution.

"Mark this bearing," said Weisig evenly. "Load torpedo bays one and two." From this point on, Weisig never took his eyes off the target. The chance that it would make a random turn or a preplanned zigzag forced him to wait until the last possible moment before giving the order to shoot. "Range 1,000 meters." He gave some orders to modify the trim of the boat and to refine the bearing. They were running on the electric motors, which meant their speed was greatly reduced from that on the surface, and Weisig had to act with both precision and speed, or he could quickly lose his opportunity. "Hold steady . . . steady . . ." Then, with a triumphant lift in his voice, "Fire one!"

The ship shuddered as the blast of compressed air launched the torpedo out of its tube and into the cold waters of the Atlantic Ocean. Its compressed-air engine started it on a straight line at the incredible speed of thirty-six knots, which would continue until it either hit the target with 436 pounds of high explosives or until it missed the target, in which case it would keep going until it ran out of air, leaving it to sink irretrievably to the bottom of the ocean.

"Time 17:50:05," said Braun, who had activated his stopwatch the moment the torpedo left the tube. "Torpedo running!"

"Fire two!"

This time the chief of the boat started a second stopwatch. With any luck, one of the two torpedoes would strike home. With superb skill and a generous helping of luck, both would hit, but just one was enough.

Weisig pulled back from the periscope tube for a moment and rubbed his eyes. He leaned forward again. With the distance from the target, the approximate travel time of the torpedo to target would be a little less than two minutes.

"They've spotted our first torpedo. Men are scrambling on the deck, and the captain has turned away."

"Will they evade it?" one of the new men asked breathlessly—not yet aware that it was against protocol to speak at moments like this.

"They can turn all they want," replied Braun, "but their fate is now sealed. Either we fired a winning shot or we didn't. There is nothing they can do to change their fate."

The answer wasn't long in coming as Weisig recoiled from the viewfinder—the flash of a torpedo exploding in the near dark was enough to hurt his eyes even at that distance.

Before he could announce their success, a low thump rumbled against the hull of the ship. "A direct hit by number one!" Weisig shouted. He repeated this into the speaking tube connecting the bridge to the torpedo room, which caused an instant huzzah by the crew of the number-one tube.

When Weisig recoiled a second time, even Braun let out an excited cheer.

Weisig turned and grinned. "We blew off their bow and stern. That ship is going to have a problem figuring out which end ought to sink first!" He was gratified to hear them all laugh. Any despondency from the crew over their previous failures had now completely dissipated.

"Prepare to surface!" The men sprang into action to adjust the various valves and levers that would send compressed air into the ballast tanks to create the buoyancy needed for their rise to the surface. When the all-clear was sounded, Weisig ordered, "Surface!" and the helmsman quickly changed the attitude of the forward planes to adjust the ship's movement. In what seemed a matter of moments, the ship breached the surface, and the conning tower crew quickly cleared and opened the scuttles so the captain could come on deck. "Gun crews to your mounts!" he ordered, and then he quickly pulled himself on deck, followed by Braun.

"Oh, my," said Braun.

Weisig nodded. "What a scene of horror." By now the last light of twilight was fading from the sky so that the flames that were boiling out of the hatches of the doomed freighter lit up the night sky in an eerie and awful dance of death that was punctuated by the cries of burning men.

"Many will perish without making it out of the hull. The fact that the ship is still floating indicates that they sealed the watertight bulkhead doors—they trapped their own crew below the waterline."

Braun found it amazing that his captain could say this with no apparent emotion. The guns crew had prepared their guns and were standing by. Weisig intended to give the men on the freighter plenty of time to make it into the lifeboats and would then determine whether the ship was sinking rapidly enough on its own or if he should order some shots below the waterline to speed the process. But just at that moment there was a noticeable twang on the metal skin of the ship below them, followed quickly by another.

"What the . . ." said Braun, astonished. "They're shooting at us with small weapons." Instinctively he crouched a bit but not out of cowardice.

"The fools!" Weisig leaned over the cowling and shouted to the men on the forward gun, "Fire a shot across their bows. Then reload for a shot into the bridge! Fire when ready."

This was the sort of thing a gun crew lived for. All the hours of tedious practice and maintenance were now about to pay off. With the highly skilled training that was characteristic of every German military man, regardless of the branch of service, they quickly brought their gun to bear, followed by a ten-foot muzzle blast and a distinct crack that echoed across the water. The effect on the American ship was immediate as the person responsible for shooting from their deck quickly threw his gun into the water and then held up his hands.

"Stand down!" called Weisig to the gun crew. Then with a smile, he said, "A fool—but a brave one. I'd like to think I might fight back if the situation were reversed."

By this point the American ship had started settling with a distinct list to the port side. Because the number of crew on a steamer was relatively small, most of the men who could escape were already in the water. "I don't think any further shelling will be necessary," said the captain. "That ship will be fully underwater in another ten minutes and couldn't be saved even if the British managed to get here with a warship. Let's give it another minute or two and then withdraw."

Braun surveyed the scene—a large American trawler wallowing in the ocean, flames pouring out of it. With a single torpedo hit it could sometimes take up to an hour for a ship to sink, but with a double hit, this boat was clearly doomed. By this point the shouts of burning men had faded, replaced by cries of help from those who had jumped, or been blasted, directly into the water. The Germans could see the men in the lifeboats working to find their comrades in the water.

"If war were sane, we'd shoot all of them, you know."

Braun whirled at this suggestion from Weisig. "Pardon me?"

Weisig shrugged. "It makes no sense that we sink a ship but allow the crew to survive to fight another day. If our goal is to cut England off from supplies, as they are doing to Germany, then we ought to take every possible advantage to reduce their supply of manpower."

"But the Articles of War—"

"—are obsolete. In times past you would put a hole in a ship and then invite the crew to come aboard as prisoners, where you could detain them for the balance of the war. If you were lucky, you'd even take the ship as a prize, or at least its cargo. But our accommodations are a bit too tight for any of that. So now we put them to sea, either to be rescued or to die slowly and horribly. Either way, it does nothing to help us and everything to hurt us."

"Are you going to . . ."

Weisig shook his head. "No, I'm not going to kill any of them. We haven't come to that point yet. But with tens of thousands dying in the trenches, I doubt that any of the ground commanders would feel any compunction against doing what I've suggested." He straightened up. "Prepare to dive! If there are any British destroyers lurking about, I want to be safely underwater when they arrive! My guess is that this torch that we've lit up in the night has all of them alerted, and they know that their allies from America have felt the wrath of the Kaiser's navy!" He said this both to the men on the hull as well as into the voice tube so that everyone could hear the results of their attack. He was heartened by the cheer that went up from his men.

"A nice night's work," he said to Braun.

"Yes, sir." Braun suppressed his natural response that provoking the Americans was a strategic mistake—one that could prove fatal in the long run. There would be time enough to reflect on such things when they had found their way to safety.

Chapter 2
Liverpool to New York

April 15, 1915—Liverpool, England

Looking up at the massive superstructure of the steamship *Lusitania,* Cunard Line's flagship, Annie Stringham asked quietly, "Do you put any stock in all of this talk of German submarines attacking neutral ships?"

"Not in an attack on a ship like the *Lusy,*" replied her husband, Everett. "But they have been firing torpedoes at an increasing number of armed merchant ships without any warning to the crew, including American ships." He paused. "And troopships—they've started going after the troopships. The only problem a passenger ship like *Lusitania* could face is if she's mistaken for one of the British ocean liners that have been converted to military transport ships, like the *Mauretania* and *Aquitania.*" To reduce his wife's anxiety, he added, "But you don't need to worry. Even the Germans would never attack a passenger liner, particularly not with Americans on board. Can you imagine the international outcry?"

"I think there should be an outcry because they don't give the crews of the merchant ships a chance to escape. It's barbarous . . ." Annie would have said more, but a delivery truck sounded its horn, overwhelming any attempt at conversation.

When it stopped, they overheard a couple talking nearby, the wife saying, "I've never seen anything so beautiful in my life as this ship. It's magnificent!"

"People are beautiful," whispered Annie to Everett. "Ships are just very large and noisy machines."

Everett suppressed a smile. His wife was not one to be impressed by technology, having judged that it brought as many problems as solutions. But for his part, he agreed with the young woman at the railing. The ship was beautiful—the pinnacle of modern engineering.

"Shall we go explore our stateroom?" asked Everett.

He smiled and took her arm.

* * *

"WILL YOU TAKE THIS WITH YOU?"

Bill Shafer looked down at the small book his mother held out and took it reluctantly. "I don't have a lot of room, you know. They discourage us from bringing personal items."

"I'd feel better if you had it."

"I don't know why you get all nervous when we go out of port," said Bill's older brother, Avery. "It's not like we're in the Royal Navy, where we'd actually face real danger." The tinge of bitterness in his voice was unmistakable.

"Please, let's not argue," she replied. "I know you boys want to join the navy. But my heart couldn't take it. And the government says that your service on the great ocean liners is helping England very well. We need to keep the sea lanes open."

Avery looked away and rolled his eyes but didn't reply.

"I'll take the book, Mum." Bill attempted a smile. "I may even read it, if I get a few minutes."

Clara Shafer handed the book to Bill and then gave him a light hug. "Well, then, you boys had better be off to the pier. I'm surprised they didn't have you there much earlier. I'll be glad when each of you gets to take your month off. We'll have time to talk then."

Bill didn't tell her that he planned to use his month trying to figure out how to get off the *Lusitania* and into His Majesty's Royal Navy. It really would break her heart. But England was at war, and serving as a steward on a seagoing hotel was hardly the way for an ambitious young man of twenty-two to find glory and honor. "We'll see you in a couple of weeks, Mum." Bill leaned down and gave his mother a hug and a light kiss on her cheek.

Avery, a fireman down in the engine room of the ship, was so stocky from shoveling tons of coal into the furnaces that his massively muscled arms nearly engulfed his widowed mother as he too embraced her in a full hug.

"Come back safe," she whispered quietly into his ear.

Even though Avery hated it when she talked like that—a common sailor's superstition that it brought bad luck to talk about coming back—he laughed and picked her up and off the floor to give her a good shake. "That crazy Kaiser isn't going to get me! Don't you worry about that! You just have a hot meal waiting when we get back." He was pleased to hear her laugh, and then he and Bill were out the door.

As they jogged down the street, Avery turned to Bill. "I need to stop by Mary's. Little Frankie has some kind of present for me."

"You'll be late—we barely have time to make it as it is."

"I won't be a minute." He hesitated. "It's important to Mary." Bill waited, knowing what was coming next. "Can you make some kind of excuse for me? I promise I won't be more than ten minutes."

Bill didn't know how he felt about this. After their father had died at sea, Avery had been the closest thing Bill had to a father. Now it felt as if he too was abandoning him. Of course he knew that was foolish—it was only natural that Avery would find someone to marry. But a widow with a child? Plus, he didn't like telling lies. He jogged on for a moment or two before casting a quick glance at Avery. Seeing the anxious look on his brother's face, he replied, "Sure!"

"Thanks. I owe you one!"

"You owe me a couple of dozen, you blighter!"

Avery smiled and turned at the next corner. In a few moments he came to a small cottage on an obscure lane filled with row houses. Before he could even reach the door, it flew open, and a five-year-old boy bolted out and straight into Avery's arms.

"Whoa, there!" shouted Avery, pretending to fall back from the blow. "You're going to knock me right off my feet!" The fact that Avery had the build of a healthy young ox meant that the boy couldn't possibly have knocked him off balance, but the little fellow's laughter made the feint well worth it.

Hugging Avery tightly, Frankie exclaimed, "I've got something for you to take to America."

"So your mum tells me." Avery looked up and smiled at Mary. Mary Winsel was an attractive woman, though not, perhaps, the type to win a beauty pageant. Dark hair and even darker eyes were her most prominent features. She was older than Avery by at least five years, a fact that puzzled many of his friends. But Avery had been part of the rescue party that had helped recover her husband's body from the shipwreck that had taken his life, and so it was he who had accompanied his captain to her home to deliver the bad news. At her request he attended the funeral and then started helping out with small chores around the house. And so their friendship had started. Even now Avery wasn't entirely sure what his motives were for coming back, although he did love little Frankie, which was odd, given his tough-guy reputation. His affection for Mary seemed to grow each time he saw her. As she returned his smile, beckoning him into the house, his body was flooded with warmth, and he felt unaccountably happy.

"We better hurry," he said to Frankie. "I haven't much time, and I can't wait to see what you've made for me." He carried the boy across the threshold and into the house, where the aroma of freshly baked cookies gave him an idea of what his present might be.

* * *

EVEN EVERETT WAS STARTLED AS the powerful steam horn bellowed out the first of three blasts, signaling everyone within twenty miles that the *Lusitania* was about to set sail for America. The giant horn was pitched perfectly so that its sonorous bass timbre resonated with a person's entire body, rather than just the ears, and with such ferocious intensity that the hair on the back of Everett's neck involuntarily stood on end, even when he expected the signal.

"Shall we go up on deck to watch our departure from port?" asked Annie.

"Maybe we could just telephone someone up there to tell us about it," Everett replied. He was still enthralled with the idea that every first-class cabin had its own telephone to call for service or even to connect to the other cabins. Phones weren't common in 1915, let alone on board a ship.

Annie shook her head. "A walk up the stairs will do us good . . ."

"The stairs? We should use the elevators!" That was another *Lusitania* innovation that Everett's gadget-loving mind was impressed with, but Annie furrowed her brow.

"On the other hand, the stairs would do us good." Finally she nodded in agreement.

As they made their way down the carpeted corridor, Everett cast a jealous glance at the heavily ornamented wrought-iron column enclosing the elevator shaft. The car came rising into view just as they turned to make their way up the staircase. Still, vindicating Annie, they beat the elevator to the promenade deck, where huge potted plants and trees gave the foyer the feeling of a Mediterranean seaside villa, even though they were still in chilly old England.

Everett pointed to an open spot next to the ship's railing, and soon they were resting their arms on the polished teak handrails that looked out over the side of the ship.

"Liverpool's a grimy little place, isn't it?" said Everett as they looked down on the town from nearly six stories up.

Annie nodded but chose not to reply, since she judged it rude to say such things in public. "Were you able to sign the agreements with the British government that you hoped to?"

Everett nodded. "The Liverpudlians are sharp negotiators. But in the end we all got a fair deal. I don't know how much it will help our business directly, since most of the coal they signed for will come from mines in the Eastern United States, but I suppose that leaves more domestic customers for us . . ."

"Liverpudlians?" asked Annie dubiously.

Everett smiled. "Their word, not mine. Residents of Liverpool. Just like you're an Evanstonian."

Annie laughed. "But I'm not a Wyomingian . . . at least I don't think so. Am I?"

Everett shook his head. He loved this woman for her uncommon combination of practicality mixed with playfulness.

They were interrupted by a subtle shudder underfoot. "Do you feel that?" he asked excitedly.

"What?"

"That tremor. I believe that means they've started the steam turbines. Notice how the deck is shaking, ever so slightly."

"But it's so quiet . . ."

"Quiet indeed. This will be the first time we've traveled on a ship that uses a steam turbine rather than reciprocating engines. I've heard that it makes a tremendous difference in both the noise and the smoothness of the ship's operation. It's the reason the *Lusitania* is so fast. Shipbuilders had reached the maximum speed they could with piston engines, but now they expect they can go even faster than the twenty-five knots the *Lusy*'s been clocked at. I've been excited to see if we could tell a difference."

"Well, I like that it's quiet. Isn't that the Fellowes family down there waving? Do you suppose they came to see us?"

Everett strained to sort out the people whom Annie was pointing to. The departure of an ocean liner was still a big event on both sides of the Atlantic, and hundreds of well-wishers showed up to escort the passengers on board and see them to their cabins. Then, with a final whistle, the crowd dissipated as family and friends crossed back over the gangplank to the observation deck to wave good-bye and bon voyage. "I don't think I see them, dear . . ."

"Over there—it is the Fellowes, and I'm quite certain they're waving at us!" Annie waved back while simultaneously pointing Everett in the right direction. He could see that the local branch president of the LDS Church was happy when Everett finally spied him, and Everett tipped his hat in recognition.

"But they wouldn't come down here just for us. We only attended their branch four Sundays . . ." said Annie.

"I doubt that they're here for us. It was just fortuitous that they spotted us. See, they're also waving at someone toward the stern of the ship." Everett was thoughtful. "A very good family—I'm sorry about the privations the war has imposed on them. It seems all our British members are in difficult circumstances—many on such strict rations that they're actually going hungry. But in spite of it all, they seem to stay in good cheer."

"How long do you think this war will take? Hopefully not too long."

Everett rested his hand on his wife's. Like most Americans, she was a pacifist who thought that this European war that now engulfed Great Britain, France, and Russia as allies against the Central Powers of Germany and Austria was a needless slaughter that America should stay out of at any cost.

He sighed. "I don't know. Both Germany and the Allies thought it would be over in six weeks, with their side victorious. The Germans very nearly pulled it off, you know—they reached the outskirts of Paris in just more than six weeks. But those extra few days proved their undoing when the Parisians rallied and drove them back. Now it's been eight months of horror. Right now it seems hard for either side to gain an advantage, and the troops just continue to fight from their trenches." He shrugged. "So I don't know. It may go on much longer than anyone could have imagined."

"We're starting to move now!" Annie said. In fact, they had to steady themselves as the four massive propellers bit into the water, the ship pressing forward through the channel leading them to the open sea. "Good-bye!"Annie shouted to the Fellowes just as the horn sounded again. Of course the Fellowes couldn't hear her, but they could see that she and Everett were waving and shouting to them, and that's what counted.

"I'll miss them," said Annie. "I admire how they get along here, in spite of all this adversity. You'll call on them again when you get back?"

Everett nodded. He'd hoped to wrap up the various transactions the Coal Mine Owners Association had tasked him with in time for him to return to America with Annie to see their teenaged daughter Lily enrolled in finishing school. She was among a handful of young women in Evanston, Wyoming, who had finished high school. However, the list of contracts and audits he was expected to conduct while in England was simply too long to get it all done in a single visit. So now he was accompanying Annie to New York, where he'd pair her up with her cousin and cousin's husband, who were also traveling west while he commuted back to England for perhaps another six weeks of work. Although a mine owner in his own right, Everett was an elected official of the association and had undertaken the task of trying to secure the best possible terms for the massive supply of coal used to fuel the shipping lines to England—the lifeline for the embattled British Empire. Fortunately, the Welsh mines were equal to the task of fueling British ships as they left England.

As the ship made its way northwest toward the mouth of the Mersey estuary, Everett gazed thoughtfully on the more than seven miles of docks they were passing en route to the village of Bootle and then out to the open sea. "It's humbling to think that our ancestors passed by this very spot more than half a century ago on their way to the wilderness of the Great Salt Lake valley, and not on an elegant luxury liner like the *Lusitania,* but rather on a sailing ship that took more than six weeks to cross the ocean. Think of the courage it took to leave everything behind just because of their convictions . . ."

"My aunt died on the voyage . . ."

Everett turned to Annie. "Your aunt? I didn't know that. Tell me about it."

"My mother's baby sister, Elizabeth. There was a terrible storm that raged in the North Atlantic for more than a week. My mother was just a little girl, but she remembers how sick everyone was. Little Lizzie, as they called her, simply couldn't hold any food down and stopped nursing. They watched helplessly as life faded from her little body."

"What did they do when she died?"

"The only thing they could do—they buried her at sea. My grandmother never really got over it. But Mama told me that whenever the subject came up, my grandmother would quickly say that they'd do it all again for the gospel. She took great comfort in the fact that little children are saved, even without baptism." Annie brushed a tear from her cheek. "I'm sure that Grandma's in heaven raising that little girl even now." Everett patted her hand. The cost for the early Saints had been high.

"Look," said Everett, pointing, "we're past the docks. Just a little more sailing to the mouth of the Mersey and then into the Irish Sea. In less than a week, we'll be in New York City. Time to say good-bye to England."

"Good-bye, then, England!" said Annie. With the war as it was, it was impossible to know when, if ever, she'd be coming back.

Chapter 3
In the Bowels of the Monster

"You there! Watch your rhythm—live coals on the floor are unacceptable!"

"And you think that's the first time I've ever been told that, you drunken oaf?" Avery Shafer muttered to himself as he stepped away from the open furnace door where he'd just shoveled a load of black coal into the furnace, deftly swinging the door closed as he did so. This time he got it right, and the furnace door closed just as the bow of the ship started to rise. Since his furnace faced toward the front of the ship, the trick was to shovel the coal into the furnace while the bow of the ship was dipping into the trough of a wave and then slam the door shut before it started to rise on the leading side of a new wave. That way gravity worked for you rather than against you. Open the door at the right time, and gravity sucked the new coal deep into the furnace where it instantly flamed into life. Open it at the wrong time, and you risked having a sheet of white-hot coals come cascading back out of the furnace onto the floor where the fresh coal was waiting to be shoveled in. Not only did that burn workers' feet and add to the misery of the already-suffocating heat of the place, but it was sure to bring a reprimand to the poor fireman who allowed it to happen. He'd have to spend his time returning the coals that were lost instead of adding new fuel to the fire. In foul weather, the rise and fall of the ship could be as great as sixty feet, which meant that gravity was more than able to trip up the fireman who failed to judge his timing just perfectly. "As if we know when the ship is going to plow into a wave and how long it will last, since we have such a great view down here below the waterline . . ." Avery certainly didn't need to whisper as he added this commentary. The noise in the furnace room was a constant cacophony of men grunting and cursing as one thousand tons of coal was being directed into place by the trimmers so it could be heaved into the furnaces by the grimy human troglodytes turned firemen. Add to that the feral roar of the fires that burned white-hot along the length of grates at the bottom of the nearly two hundred furnaces. Each furnace vaporized the water into superheated steam within the bowels of the massive boilers.

"Put your back into it, Shafer!" The only thing Avery hated more than coal at this particular moment were the supervisors who watched over the more than 300 trimmers and firemen who, with their human muscle and sinew, kept the inferno raging twenty-four hours a day deep inside the lower decks of the ship.

"Yes, sir!" he shouted as he threw another shovelful of coal into the furnace. Glancing through the coal dust, he saw the faces of his fellow workers shining with sweat in the orange glow of the fires. The dust was so thick in the air that it almost completely obscured the electric lights overhead. Even though the work was backbreaking and sure to wreck his health in the long run, he really did love it down here. Whether they knew it or not, everyone else on board the ship, passengers and crew alike, were absolutely dependent on him—lowly Avery Shafer—for their very survival. If the fires ever went out, the *Lusitania* would be nothing more than a great hulk of metal foundering helplessly in the ocean.

* * *

"OH, MY!"

"It's not often that you're left speechless, my dear."

"Do you blame me?" asked Annie. "I've certainly never seen anything quite like this in my life. Do you see that dome? It's magnificent! And on a ship at sea."

Everett looked up at the huge plaster dome, rising some thirty feet above their heads in the first-class dining saloon, and marveled at its intricate moldings and hand-painted artwork. It was the ultimate expression of James Millar's extravagant architecture displayed throughout the *Lusitania,* particularly in the first-class areas, including the dining saloon, the library, and the lounge.

"I'm not sure," said Everett mischievously. "I think I like the dome in the first-class lounge more—particularly when the sun illuminates the stained-glass panels in the ceiling. There are twelve of them, one glass panel for each month of the year."

"It's really too much," said Annie. "Just how do they build something like this on a ship that has so much motion? It seems like it would crack the plaster."

The Stringhams had entered the first-class dining saloon from the upper deck. The room was huge, more than eighty-five feet long and eighty-two feet across and occupying two full decks. It easily enclosed a space far larger than all but a few of the greatest dining halls in the world. From the upper portico they were presented with a mezzanine view that widened to an oval area in the center of the room, opening the space between the upper and lower deck of the dining hall with a large circular staircase. Fashionable Greek pillars supported the dome overhead. The opening to the lower level was surrounded by an intricate wrought-iron railing, painted white, with highly polished teak handrails for guests who wished to look down on the fashionably dressed ladies and gentlemen who were arriving for their evening meal. Gold-monogrammed medallions were distributed tastefully around the railing with the large letter C for "Cunard." The overall effect was striking enough to make you forget that the whole scene took place in the midships of a great ocean liner, rather than the grand dining hall of some European palace.

"Oh, Everett. This really is more than we need. I mean, really . . ."

"Well, it was extravagant to book first class, but what else is money for? Sad to say, but the war has been good for our coal business, so I don't think it's unreasonable that we enjoy the crossing."

By now they'd reached the head waiter's pedestal. "Welcome aboard, Mr. and Mrs. Stringham. My name is Alain, and it will be my pleasure to see to your comfort and service. May I escort you to your table?" Everett nodded, and Alain walked ahead of them as they made their way toward a table at the back of the upper level.

As they approached their table, Everett turned back for a quick look, deciding that everything about the room was perfect, from the masterfully finished white-enameled wood panels on the walls to the richly polished mahogany tables. Even the deep knap of the carpets was the same color as the beautifully fitted upholstery on the chairs.

As they reached their table, Alain paused another moment. "Perhaps I can introduce you to your fellow diners, since you'll be sharing the same table throughout the voyage." There were two other couples at the table. To those already seated at the table, Alain said formally, "First, may I present Mr. and Mrs. Everett Stringham from Evanston, Wyoming, in the United States."

Everett tipped his head slightly, aware that the reaction on the other diners' faces would have been little different if Alain had announced that the Stringhams were from the planet Mercury in the inner orbit of the solar system. The mere mention of the word *Wyoming* often had that effect on people since most thought it was still the Wild West with shoot-outs and cowboy hats and Indian teepees. While the cowboy-hat part was still mostly true, Wyoming was very much part of the twentieth century, and quite socially advanced at that—the first in the nation to grant women the right to vote, for example—a right still not granted nationally. But few people knew anything about Wyoming, and Everett did his best not to smile.

Alain simply continued. "To your right are Sir William and Lady Baxter of London." Sir William stood and bowed slightly to Annie. "And next to the Baxters are Mr. and Mrs. Anderson of, correct me if I'm in error, Newton, Massachusetts." Mrs. Anderson looked not the least impressed, neither by the setting nor by the Stringhams, and barely acknowledged the introduction. Her husband was of a very different temperament, however, and he smiled broadly. "Pleased to meet you." He stood up and stepped around the table to shake Everett's hand.

"We'll be pleased to share a table with all of you," said Everett diplomatically. If the earlier reaction of the other table guests bothered him, it didn't register on his face or in his voice.

Alain held the chair for Annie while their earlier-introduced table waiter, Geoffrey, pulled a chair out for Everett. "May I help you with your napkin," he asked before Everett could make the mistake of reaching for it on his own. Unfolding it with a flourish, Geoffrey snapped it into his lap with a single sweeping motion that made it seem like the most natural thing in the world.

"Thank you." Everett smiled, deciding that a smile was better than laughing.

As they sat down, Annie found a moment when no one was looking to wink at Everett. Leaning close to her, he whispered, "Pardon me, madam, but I believe you were admiring the cut of my evening jacket."

"You caught me, then?" And then more quietly, "By the reaction of our fellow diners, this could turn out to be a long voyage—at least during dinner."

* * *

"Be quick about it, now. You have to turn the beds down before the family returns from dinner."

Bill Shafer nodded. "Do you think they'll stop for entertainment or cards?"

"That is not our concern," replied his managing steward. "Invisible. That's what you need to be—invisible. That is, unless they specifically seek you out to make a request, in which case you treat them with courtesy and tact. Greet them by name when they come across you, but do your best to remain out of sight when possible. I'm sure you understand . . ."

There was a time when all this had irritated Bill. After all, it was hardly his first crossing, and he'd been through this particular lecture a dozen times before. But he'd finally decided that his supervisor, John Todd, was the type of person who simply had to be in control of all situations and who would always treat those who worked under him as inferiors. It was just how he placed himself in the world, so it did no good for Bill to get out of sorts over it, since it would be impossible for Todd to change.

"Yes, sir. Invisible it is."

Todd tipped his head and looked at Bill, perhaps trying to decide if he was sincere or simply indulging him. If it were the latter, Todd would be irritated. But Bill held his gaze steady and displayed not the least sign of irony, so Todd acknowledged him and moved on to torment some other room steward.

As the door closed, Bill breathed a sigh of relief and said, "That's much better." He spoke this out loud since he liked to talk to himself when he was alone. It helped make the job pass more quickly. Being a steward was, in many regards, a solitary occupation since he had to operate behind the scenes. And it could be very stressful since those who paid the princely sums required to stay in first class had very definite opinions about how they should be catered to. That's why he had fewer suites to care for than he did when working in second class. The rooms were not only larger, but vastly better appointed, and all of it required dusting and polishing, sweeping and scrubbing. This particular suite comprised a spacious bedroom, a sitting room, and a bathroom. A second-class room on the *Lusitania* was the equivalent of most first-class cabins on any other ship, which meant the first-class cabins had to be even more extravagant than usual. Caring for it all was a hard job that required a lot of stamina: lifting the heavy linens from the bed, picking up thc clothes that his assigned guests often left strewn about the floor, and generally bringing order to their untidiness. Many first-class passengers brought their valets and housekeepers along, which had its own set of problems. These permanent servants tended to look down on the ship's stewards as standing on a lower rung of the social ladder than they—which is why he was glad that the Stringhams were on their own and that he could work uninterrupted in their behalf.

* * *

ANNIE LOOKED AT THE MENU in alarm. On the one hand, it was absolutely beautiful, printed in color with grand images of sailing ships and the Statue of Liberty, presided over by the crest of the Cunard Steamship Company set in a gilded crescent surrounded by two elegantly dressed classical ladies in red and green dresses. But it was the menu itself that was intimidating. Leaning close to Everett, she whispered, "I don't know what all of these mean!" The menu included dishes like *tortue verte, suprême de sole, chipolata,* and *gâteaux mexicaine.*

"Just be calm. European style is to eat the salad at the end of the meal, rather than the beginning. You enjoy both beef and fish, so choose between the *sole* and sirloin for your main entree. And then we'll worry about dessert later."

Annie took a deep breath. "All right. I'll follow your lead."

After placing their orders, Sir William Baxter broke the ice on the conversation. "So, Mr. Stringham, I'm afraid to confess that I know very little about Wyoming. Perhaps you could enlighten us?"

"We're located in the western United States in the Rocky Mountains. It's actually a very beautiful setting with high-mountain deserts and magnificent granite mountains to the south of us that rival the Alps in beauty and size. We even have the red-rock canyons of the Green River before it joins the Colorado."

"Really? I had no idea. And would it be permissible for me to ask what you are engaged in out there?"

"I own a number of coal mines. Wyoming and Utah are home to some large coal reserves, and my family has been involved in that for nearly half a century now." With this revelation, the expression on Baxter's face changed considerably.

"That is very interesting. It turns out my family has some history with coal. Perhaps we could chat about it sometime during the voyage?"

"Of course. I'd be happy to." Everett's expression showed that he was pleased by this interchange.

"And what about you, Mr. Anderson? Is there coal in Massachusetts? I'm afraid that all I know about your state is that they had that rather nasty business about tea in the Boston Harbor some years ago." Sir William said this with an impish smile. Annie decided that her earlier indictment might prove wrong and that dining with these people might be entertaining after all.

Anderson laughed. "No coal where we live. I'm in the automobile business."

"What kind of cars do you make?" asked Everett. "I just purchased a Pierce-Arrow town car, the first in automobile in our small town."

"Very nice," said Anderson. "Pierce-Arrow is certainly a leader. I work for the Stanley Motor Carriage Company where I'm first vice president for sales."

"The Stanley Steamer? I thought very seriously of purchasing one myself. Quite an impressive speed record you've set."

"More than 130 miles per hour—and with marvelous torque to boot!" It seemed Anderson was the type who beamed when saying something that excited him.

"I was concerned about the safety—a steam boiler mounted directly behind the driver. Seems like it might get a bit dangerous if the boiler overheated."

"There are safety valves everywhere. And joints that would rupture long before the boiler. It's actually one of the safest automobiles on the road."

There was the briefest of lulls in the conversation, which gave Annie the opportunity she hoped for. She was convinced that her husband and Mr. Anderson could fill the rest of the evening with this automobile chatter, so she quickly joined the conversation. "And may I ask about you, Sir William? You hold a distinguished title."

Baxter smiled and bowed his head. "I'm retired military. British Army. A Baxter family tradition. Presently I'm on a trade mission to the United States on behalf of the government to negotiate supplies for our war effort. That's why your husband's business may be of some interest."

"If you don't mind my being so bold," interjected Anderson, "I'd be interested to know how one becomes a knight in England." When he saw the look of horror on his wife's face, he quickly added, "I'm sure I should know that, and if you'd rather not say . . ."

Baxter quickly put him at ease. "I don't mind at all. I'm sure it's not as grand as it sounds. The king chooses a number of individuals each year on whom to bestow a title. It can be for any number of reasons, including success in business that furthers British interests, an unusual accomplishment in the arts, or, in my case, for the exploits of a military career. It's nothing, really."

"My husband is too modest," said Lady Baxter. "He is actually a Knights Commander of the Order of the Bath, an order of chivalry that dates back nearly two hundred years. King Edward invested him with this honor for his excellent military service in South Africa."

Before they could engage in further conversation, their waiter Geoffrey arrived with appetizers and began to quickly place the fine china settings in front of the guests.

"Off to a nice start," Annie whispered to Everett. He was relieved that she enjoyed the group, since he'd worried about putting them in first class. Her commonsense practicality could sometimes be offended by such a setting. He squeezed her hand and smiled as he started into the *crême chatillon.*

* * *

With a satisfied expression, Bill Shafer stepped to the door of the last of the three staterooms he was responsible for. All was in order, and he could finally go to bed. Thinking he was alone, he clicked off the electric lights in the Stringhams' suite and backed his way into the hall, where he promptly collided with Annie Stringham.

"Excuse me!" she said, stepping back.

Bill turned in alarm and was horrified when he realized he'd backed into a passenger—particularly a woman.

"Sorry." He blushed. "I'm very sorry, I was just . . ."

"It's all right. I'm fine." She smiled warmly.

"I'm still very sorry, I should have looked."

"No harm done," said Mr. Stringham.

"Thank you, Mr. Stringham." He then looked at Mrs. Stringham and nodded. "Mrs. Stringham. My name is Shafer—Bill Shafer, your cabin steward. I hope you'll find that everything is in order."

"Pleased to meet you," said Mrs. Stringham.

"Very good to meet you, Bill. You work on a magnificent ship."

"Yes, sir. Thank you." He backed to other side of the hallway. "I'm here at your service for the duration of the voyage. If you need anything—anything at all—you should call me on the telephone no matter what time of day or night it is. I left my card on your night table."

Mr. Stringham nodded. "Thank you. But I doubt that anything will be so urgent that we need to get you up in the night. I've watched how hard you stewards work. It really is demanding, isn't it?"

"Yes, sir. But still, most guests are far from reticent in calling when they need something. We expect it." He felt like he was jabbering on, all the while hearing the voice of John Todd in his head proclaiming, *Invisible . . . we should be invisible . . .*

"Well, then, I'll beg your pardon and be about my business. Can I bring you some ice or anything?"

"No, that will be fine. Thank you."

Turning one last time toward Mrs. Stringham, he said, "Sorry, again, ma'am. I hope I didn't hurt you."

"I'm all right. Really. Don't mention it again." Annie smiled, and Bill felt himself relax. He held the door open as the Stringhams entered their stateroom.

After they closed the door, he took a deep breath. "Glad John Todd wasn't here to see that!"

* * *

ANNIE MADE HER WAY TO the dressing table where she started to take off her jewelry. "I think it's exciting that you get to meet with Sir William tomorrow. It's not every day you get to talk with royalty."

"He's not royalty. But he is well placed. And I'm interested in what he wants to know about our coal."

Annie stood and asked Everett to unbutton the back of her dress. "I guess this will go better than I had imagined," she said. "I thought everyone would be stuffy and judgmental, but the Baxters seem quite gracious."

"They've been trained in good manners all their lives. Even if they didn't care for us, they'd never show it."

"That Mr. Anderson is quite a character."

Everett smiled. "Yes, I doubt we'll ever lack for conversation." He stepped forward and hugged his wife. "I miss you already. It will be hard to say good-bye when we get to New York."

"So let's not think about that just now," she said as she switched off the light.

* * *

AVERY SHAFER FELL INTO THE small bunk that was far too little for his powerful frame. "I am so exhausted!"

"So shut your trap, then!" He shared the room with another fireman and two trimmers. They had all worked their two four-hour shifts just like Avery and were undoubtedly every bit as worn out as he was. Between them they had moved literally tons of coal that day.

"It's always hardest the first day, isn't it?" Avery didn't care if he bothered them. He was not the type to fall right asleep at night, and he needed time to unwind. But when no one answered, he decided not to annoy them anymore. As he put his hand out to the side of his bunk, he could feel the cold, damp plating of the inner hull situated below the waterline. Connected to the outer hull by struts that conducted the frigid temperature of the Atlantic, the inner wall was covered with condensation from the moist air in the lower decks. Avery reflected on how little separated him from the water. But he wasn't disturbed by it. He tried to think about how he could tell his mother that he was going into the navy but then wondered if he really should enlist. He did have other interests. Rolling to his side he spied the simple little pencil sketch that Frankie had drawn for him. It was the rough image of a person, apparently Avery, standing high on the bridge of a large ship. It looked as if he were waving good-bye to a girl and little boy standing on the dock. Written under the picture in Mary's beautiful calligraphy were the words she said Frankie dictated himself: "Come home to us." The sketch had been Frankie's gift along with a bag of warm biscuits from Mary.

Avery sighed. Regardless of what he and Mary thought about their relationship, it was clear that Frankie wanted a dad in his life. Going off to the navy would be another blow to the little boy. He pondered whether that was a fair thing to do to a boy who had already been hurt, but it was all too complicated for his tired brain right at the moment. In a surprisingly short time he fell asleep to the sounds of the ship: water passing by as they glided through the ocean, the sound of the high pressure steam coursing through the pipes overhead, and the constant throb of the propellers in the water. They were the most comforting sounds in the world.

Chapter 4
Breakthrough

"We need to surface to get some fresh air," said Weisig.

"Yes, sir!" said First Officer Braun. They had been running submerged for hours while hiding from a British destroyer that had passed within binocular range, and the air in the ship was dank, stale, and stifling. Braun moved forward to the control room to give the order, while Weisig remained behind in the cramped quarters of the galley where he sat at a table drinking a dark German lager with his chief engineer, Rudolf Heinze.

"So what do you think of the news from the battlefront at Ypres?" asked Weisig.

"From what I heard before we left port, the result was less than satisfying. They had hoped for a breakthrough, but their hope was quickly stifled. Do you know more than me?"

Weisig shook his head. "A grand opportunity wasted. Still, the use of chlorine gas did produce an initial advantage. From what I've heard, the French were terrified by it and broke ranks and ran."

"I doubt they had any choice. I smelled chlorine gas once in a chemistry assignment that went awry. It's noxious in the extreme. When inhaled, it immediately attacks the lining of the throat and lungs, which quickly fill with liquid. Too much and a person literally drowns in their own body. Even the small amount I encountered caused me to froth around the mouth. Survivors will likely never have full lung capacity again." Heinze was thoughtful. "I would certainly run if I saw the yellow cloud approaching. I hope that doesn't make me a coward."

"No, no, of course not. The French behaved exactly as they should. Which is why this may be such an important advance. If we can overwhelm the enemy with this new weapon, perhaps we can force an early end to the war before the British starve us."

"But the French regrouped and the salient failed—what makes you think it will succeed the next time?"

Weisig leaned back against the wall and lit up a cigarette. "It failed because we were unprepared to press the advantage. A friend of mine in Berlin told me that our own officers were as surprised by how effective it was as were the French, and they simply didn't have the reserves to move forward when the gap appeared in the French lines. Four miles! Can you imagine how many troops we could have poured through a gap of four miles? Some have speculated that we could have broken the entire line."

"That would have been glorious, indeed. Of course, the British are howling again at how inhumane we are. It is a strong escalation . . ." Heinze's voice trailed off as he worried that this might sound unpatriotic.

Weisig turned to Heinze, for whom he had sincere respect, as Heinze was one of the most technically competent engineers in the fleet. "You can relax, Rudolf. I understand your concerns about the use of this gas. The world is going crazy over it. But you do know that the French were the first to use poison gas, not Germany?"

"I wasn't aware of that."

"In the very first days of the war. They lobbed canisters of tear gas at our troops, so we are simply giving back what they gave us."

"Returning with a vengeance—chlorine gas is lethal while tear gas is an irritant."

"Does that bother you?"

"Bother me? Why would it bother me—a man who spends his days and nights in the back end of a submarine smelling diesel fumes and battery acid? You ask me that after we've spent hours in this stinking-rotten air because the British are out to kill us?" He shook his head. "I have no sympathy for the French. If they don't like it, they can yield. They are the ones who mobilized against Germany and who want to steal back Alsace-Lorraine."

"That's just how I see it. I can't understand why the Americans are making so much out of this. They say it's a vicious escalation—but trench warfare is vicious, with tens of thousands of loyal Germans dying monthly. If we can press an advantage that brings an early end to the war, how can we be blamed?"

"We can't. And as far as I'm concerned, the Americans should butt out, and the British should keep their mouths shut! They have no business in the war, anyway. They claim they were coming to the rescue of the Belgians and that we violated their neutrality. But it was really just an excuse to drive Germany down. We would have passed through Belgium in a matter of weeks, and then they could have returned to their precious neutrality. Instead, England came into the war and slowed our advance. Rather than ending the war in six weeks, as planned, it has dragged on for more than eight months now." Heinze shook his head in disgust. "So whatever they are suffering is their own fault, not ours."

"Exactly," said Weisig, leaning forward as he expressed himself. "Which is also why I have no patience when . . ." He hesitated, obviously forcing himself to swallow the words he'd intended to speak, which very likely included the name of his first officer. "Which is why I have no patience when people, even experienced military officers, challenge the decision to wage all-out war on the seas. If we find a target, we will sink it."

"Of course. And it is my duty and pleasure to see that you have the power you need to do that."

"Pacifists think they are virtuous, when in reality they simply complicate things and slow down the natural course of events. Their whining leads to more casualties." There was a huge outward gush of putrid air as the watertight doors opened. In a moment, a reverse wave of fresh, cool air swept past them as the diesel engines fired into life, sucking in the outside air in great quantity. Weisig sat back again and smiled. "Nothing quite like a breath of fresh air, is there?"

"Not something I get to enjoy very often."

"Well, hopefully the French will realize what a blessing it is to breathe good air and they will fall back at our next advance. Sometimes an overpowering weapon is a kindness when it brings an early end to hostilities. That's all our leaders are trying to do—end the war before millions die."

"I'll drink to that."

Weisig raised his glass and returned the toast. "Good. Then we see eye-to-eye."

Heinze rose to his feet. "I should return to my station and supervise the recharging of the batteries. With your permission, sir."

"Permission granted."

Heinze made his way down the corridor, casting just a single glance behind him, where he saw Weisig nursing his glass, still apparently absorbed in his thoughts about the war.

Chapter 5

A Troublesome Business

"Why, there's Captain Turner." Sir William waved toward the captain, who noticeably shrugged but still changed course and came directly to them. "He hates first-class passengers, you know. He once called us all a load of bloody monkeys who are constantly chattering and who expect to be pandered to. He seldom sits at the captain's table because of it." Sir William laughed. "The irony is that the more he snubs us, the more people want to sail on his ship—just for the remote chance of actually getting to meet the old codger."

"So, why is he coming over to us?"

"Has to. My department does a great deal of work with Cunard. He'll be civil enough. But don't be surprised if he's a bit gruff."

"Good morning, Sir William. A fine day to be at sea. I'm glad you can sail with us again."

"A fine day, indeed, Captain, although it feels as if we're going a bit slower than usual."

Turner scowled. "I'm afraid that's true. The admiralty has ordered us to reduce our fuel consumption, probably on your orders. But you shouldn't despair—we can still make a comfortable twenty-two knots, which will get you to New York City in better time than any of our competitors."

"Of course." Baxter smiled. "Allow me to present Mr. Everett Stringham of . . ."

"Evanston, Wyoming."

"Yes, that's it! Evanston, Wyoming. He and I have just been discussing the coal business. It seems that he owns some coal fields out in the western United States."

"Really! Well, I wish we could get some of your coal so I could stop our regular passengers from badgering me about our speed."

Everett extended his hand to Captain Turner and smiled.

"I wish you could too. Our coal is remarkably low in sulfur and could minimize the soot coming out of those funnels of yours."

"It's dirtier than ever, isn't it? Wartime restrictions have impacted quality. How is the coal business in the States?"

"In quite a slump the past few years, although there has been a noticeable increase in orders recently because of the war."

"A thousand tons a day. That's what we need to reach top speed. Nothing happens on board without the burning of coal." Turner shifted uncomfortably. "Of course, we're trying to economize, wherever possible, as I said."

"I know it's usually against regulations, Captain, but given Mr. Stringham's professional interest in the subject, I was wondering if we might not have a look at the boiler room. I think he'd find it fascinating how the coal is stored and manipulated on the ship."

Turner's eyes widened. "Certainly not! A passenger in the mechanical areas? Cunard would have my stripes before we stepped off the boat in New York City."

Baxter smiled. "Well, it was worth a try. I was actually using Mr. Stringham for my own purposes, since I've always desperately wanted a tour of the power plant."

Turner could see that he wasn't going to get out of this easily, so he motioned for the two to sit down. "It's really impossible. But I can tell you about it. And perhaps there is something special I can do for you. The coal is stored in bunkers that are situated between the outer and inner hulls. There are also bunkers above the boilers, which means the men down there are essentially surrounded by coal. Our trimmers are responsible for extracting the coal from the various bunkers in an orderly fashion so the load stays balanced and we can maintain the trim of the ship."

"Why two hulls?" asked Everett.

"For safety purposes. In the unlikely event that the outer hull was breached, we could immediately seal that area by closing the bulkhead doors and thus contain the flooding. The interior of the ship would never have seawater."

"And once the steam is made?" asked Sir William.

"It travels through extremely high-pressure lines into the engine room, which is separate from the boiler rooms. There it feeds into four Parsons steam turbines, one for each of the four shafts, which generate a combined power output of 68,000 horsepower. The turbines turn the four screws—propellers—to provide forward thrust to the ship." He paused. "I should have added that there are actually four smaller turbines—eight total—to provide reverse power."

"Impressive . . ." said Everett.

Turner clearly liked this line of conversation, as he added, "An interesting detail that still surprises me, and that gives some sense of the power involved, is that it takes 65,000 gallons of water *per minute* to cool the equipment."

"Indeed. And you won the Blue Riband for fastest Atlantic crossing . . ." said Sir William.

"Of course, it's been taken from us by the somewhat newer ships in Cunard service, but the day *Lusitania* first took it back from the cursed Germans—after however many years their Hamburg-Amerikan Line held it—was a great day for Britain. Our fastest reported speed is 25.88 knots. If we could do that consistently, we'd have you to New York in four days instead of five."

Sir William stood up, fully aware that he'd gained more of the captain's time than most passengers could ever hope for. "It would actually be a shame to make it in four days, since that would be one less day to enjoy the superb service of your staff and crew."

Captain Turner and Everett followed his lead and both stood as well. "Yes, well, I hope the staff is treating you well. Pleased to meet you, Mr. Stringham. Enjoy the passage."

"Thank you, sir."

As Captain Turner turned to walk away, Sir William added, "You mentioned that you may be able to do something special for us?"

The captain hesitated then turned back. "Yes, I did. Since you were patient enough to let me rattle on about the ship, perhaps you'd like a tour of the bridge. I can let you safely into that area."

"I'd like that very much," Everett replied quickly.

"That would be marvelous," Sir William agreed.

"Yes? Then I'll have my first officer contact you about it. Now, good day, gentlemen. I need to go down to the engine room to meet with my chief engineer." Turner tipped his hat and quickly strode away with such a determined look on his face that no other passengers in the first-class lounge dared to interrupt him again.

As Everett and Baxter sat back down, the Englishman laughed. "Well, that's one to tell my friends about. I actually had a few paragraphs' worth of conversation with old Bowler Bill."

"Bowler Bill?"

"He's really quite a legend in the Cunard roster. He went to sea at age thirteen and was shipwrecked on his very first voyage out and very nearly drowned. Later he led a rescue party after another ship he was serving on accidentally rammed and sunk a much smaller vessel. Still later he won the heart of sailors everywhere when he jumped into the freezing-cold water of the Alexandra dock to rescue a fourteen-year-old boy who had fallen in the water. He has more awards for that type of bravery than nearly anyone in the service. At any rate, he's now the senior captain for Cunard, in spite of his rather rough temperament."

"But why 'Bowler Bill'?"

"An odd habit of the captain. Whenever he goes ashore, he puts on a bowler hat. He's done it for years. He conducts all official business with that hat of his."

Everett laughed. "I have to tell you that this time together has been delightful, although I don't know that we accomplished much. My coal is still destined for use on railroad trains in the West and can't really help you all that much."

"Actually, it will. America is going to play an important role in this war, even as a neutral country. Fortunately, your President Wilson has chosen to trade with England, which comes at the expense of Germany. I'm glad to know that as industrial demand ramps up, your country has adequate energy to meet the need."

"I'm sure we're equal to the task." Everett stood. "Now, much as I enjoy this, I'm afraid I'm neglecting my wife. I hope you'll excuse me."

"Of course. We'll see you at dinner, then." The two men shook hands and made their way to their own apartments.

* * *

Embden, Germany

"WEISIG!"

Weisig glanced to the other side of the saloon to see who it was that belonged to the voice shouting his name. "Ah—my old friend, Lieutenant Schweiger."

"Is he really an old friend?" asked First Officer Braun.

Weisig shook his head. "You can be so naive. Of course he's not my friend—just an overly ambitious U-boat captain who wants to taunt me."

"Weisig! You owe me a drink!"

Weisig stood up from the bar stool. "Come with me, Braun. I need you to keep me from doing something stupid." With that he started across the hall to the table where Schweiger and some of his cohorts were seated at a table.

"Hello, Walther. You must have had an extra drink or two. Otherwise you'd realize that it is you who owes me!"

"Really? And how do you figure that? We had three kills on our last voyage. And you had just two—one a tiny fishing boat, as I recall." The others at Schweiger's table laughed.

"You are right, of course. Except that our second kill was an American steamer, which had a greater displacement than your three targets added together. Since the Fatherland is most interested in how much enemy tonnage gets sunk, we easily win the bet."

One of Schweiger's men started to get up to challenge Weisig. He could tell this young officer in Schweiger's command was anxious for a fight. But before he could do anything, Schweiger quite wisely reached out and pulled him back down into his chair. "Sit down, Kraus. It may be that our dear friend here is right."

"What! But we got three kills!"

Schweiger motioned for Weisig and Braun to pull up a chair. "It's my mistake, really. I should know better than to enter into a bet with a former accountant unless I have all the terms of the deal spelled out perfectly in advance." He smiled a humorless smile and motioned for the barmaid to come over. "A drink for my comrades—whatever they wish."

"Very decent of you, Walther," said Weisig. "I'll buy the next round." Braun ordered a dark German beer, while Weisig asked for some hot lemon water.

"Lemon water?" asked Schweiger, an eyebrow raised.

"An unsettled stomach. Besides, I'm not much for alcohol. Never acquired a taste for it."

"Well, you are a serious fellow, aren't you? What do you do for fun?"

"I dream up ways to beat my fellow students from the academy. If you beat me on tonnage next time, I'll claim the bet was for the highest number of kills. Beat me at that, and we'll count torpedoes launched." He smiled and tipped his cup in Schweiger's direction.

"I don't like him," said Schweiger's man, Kraus.

"And I don't like you," Braun replied darkly. Of course that very nearly brought on an altercation, but Schweiger quickly subdued it.

"Be quiet, Kraus! I want to go home just one night without having to pay reparations after you get through with the bar. The English blockade poses far less of a danger to the national treasury than your antics."

"Hmmph."

"Very eloquent." Schweiger leaned forward. "So tell me the story of this American ship you sank. At the very least you became more famous than me on this voyage, that's for certain. It was in all the newspapers—with the Germans calling it long overdue and the British and Americans calling it barbaric." Schweiger took a moment to empty his stein. "But then it was I who was called barbaric when we fired on that hospital ship in February."

"My own first officer wonders about that incident as well."

"Really?" Schweiger cast a glance toward Braun.

"My captain likes to say that," replied Braun defensively, "but he knows that I back him fully and will do whatever is required of me."

Schweiger ordered another drink. "These are troubled times. The old rules are worn out now. For my part I will leave it up to the Kaiser. He is our king and knows best what is needed to win this war . . . far more than I do."

"So what will you do if confronted by a neutral passenger ship?" asked Weisig. "It's one thing to shoot down a merchant ship, but civilians?"

"Consider this—are your mother and father not civilians? Yet King Edward orders their slow starvation. How can anyone be neutral while witnessing a life-and-death struggle? When I look through a periscope, I see only friend or foe."

"That's exactly what Captain Weisig tells us," said Braun.

"Which is why I will take any shot I can get," replied Schweiger. "Even a hospital ship. The men on that ship were fully committed to fight us just as soon as they recovered. Better to kill them at sea than to face them in another battle. Isn't that right, Kraus?" He had to yell to make himself heard above Kraus's snoring. Of course, the thick-set fellow slept right through the challenge. "A loyal sailor and good German. See how he nods his head to support his captain?" Schweiger reached over and put his hand under the man's chin and lifted it up and down a few times. Kraus didn't notice a thing as he continued his slumber.

Schweiger turned to Braun. "You must not hesitate, my friend. We are ordered to shoot enemy shipping. And in my opinion any ship that is making its way to the British Isles is enemy shipping. To show mercy to them is to add to the hardship of our friends back home. For me that is no choice."

"When do you go out next?" asked Weisig.

"April 30, when the *U-20* departs for the coasts of Ireland. There should be some fat targets making their way from America toward the Irish Sea, and with any luck we'll ram a torpedo down their bows and send them to the bottom. No questions asked."

Weisig raised his glass. "We go out a week before that. So we will have the first chance. But there are plenty of fat targets for both of us—here's to good hunting." He noticed that Braun raised his glass reluctantly, which irritated Weisig more than he expected.

"So is it tonnage or number of kills next time?" asked Schweiger.

Weisig smiled. "I'll let you know just as soon as we both return."

Schweiger laughed and touched Weisig's glass with his own.

* * *

"I love Edvard Grieg," said Annie. "I thought she did a magnificent job playing his piece, didn't you?"

"I think Lily could have played as well, if she were here."

"Perhaps," said Annie, "but she's not ready for that yet. She still needs to put some polish on her cowgirl charms."

After another sumptuous meal, Annie and Everett had stopped to listen to the entertainment. Just being tablemates with Sir William and Lady Baxter had opened new doors to them, as a number of prominent guests had come up to make their acquaintance. They'd even had a chance to meet the performer, Alice MacDonald, who was a rather famous musician with the London Symphony Orchestra.

As they opened the door to their suite, they found the light was on. Annie walked in and, surprised, said, "Oh, excuse me . . ."

"Sorry. I was just cleaning things up. I'm finished now." Bill Shafer quickly stepped away from a table where he'd been looking at something.

"I hope you had an enjoyable evening . . ." For some reason the boy seemed very flustered.

"Yes, yes, we did," said Annie. "Thank you."

"Well, I should be going, then."

As he started out the door, Annie spoke up. "But perhaps you forgot to put the book back that you were looking at."

"What?" His face flushed immediately.

"Annie?" asked Everett, a bit embarrassed that she would challenge the boy. "What are you implying?"

"I saw him looking at a small book. Then he slipped something in his pocket. I'm not trying to be confrontational, but I did see that."

The stricken look on the young man's face was enough to make her regret saying anything. He stammered for just a moment before saying, "I didn't take a book. You'll find it inside the drawer. I was just straightening things up." His look turned defiant. "I'm not a thief! You can't become a steward on the *Lusitania* unless you're absolutely trustworthy."

Now Annie became embarrassed. "Let me see." She quickly stepped to the table and opened the drawer. Sure enough, there was a book inside. Looking up, she said, "But you did slip something in your pocket."

It was clear that Bill didn't want to discuss this any further, but he could not let an accusation like that stand. "It's my book." He reached inside his trouser pocket and pulled out a book that had an identical cover to the one in the drawer, although he obscured the title. "See," he said, "it's a gift from my mum." He held the book open so that Everett could see his mother's writing.

"Bill, I'm very sorry," said Everett quickly. "You can see that the books are very similar. I'm sure that's why Annie said what she did. It was a simple mistake. I hope you'll forgive us."

"Yes. Yes, I'm very sorry—" Annie began.

"Well—" Bill started to say, but he was taken by surprise as John Todd stepped into the doorway.

"Is there a problem here? Has Mr. Shafer done something objectionable?" Todd's voice was harsh.

"No. No, there's no problem. Just a misunderstanding. His service has been superlative. There's no need to discuss it further." Everett's voice was firm and controlled as he said this.

"Well, if there's a misunderstanding, then I should see that it's cleared up. Our first-class passengers should have no problems whatsoever from the staff."

"It was my fault," said Annie. "I was mistaken . . ."

"So what is it, Shafer? What has got these people upset?"

"I was just . . . I was just cleaning their table and I happened to notice that one of their books was similar to one that I had. I was simply comparing the two when they came in."

"And we thought he had our book when it was really his own. That's all," said Annie. "We have no problem with him, and he's done nothing wrong.

"See. Here's our book. Everything is in perfect order." An expression of horror crossed Bill's face as she stepped forward and handed the book to Todd.

As he took it, he glanced at the title. "The Book of Mormon." He said this with far more emphasis than it deserved, and it was obvious to everyone in the room that he was deeply disturbed by it. Turning to Bill, he said, "You tried to take *this* book?"

"No, sir. I just put it away. It has a cover similar to one that I have, that's all." Bill was clearly miserable.

"Really, Mr. Todd, I believe that's enough," said Everett with an unusually sharp edge. "We've told you that all is in order and that the service your steward has rendered is exemplary. There is no need for an investigation. Now, if you'll please leave us, this is all becoming disturbing to my wife."

Todd looked at all of them, his lips pursed white. "Well, then, we'll be off. I'm very sorry for the disturbance. I bid you all good night."

With that, he and Bill stepped out into the hall, with Todd closing the door rather sharply behind them. Everett stepped to the side of the door and listened.

"What do you think you were doing in there? You have no right to go through their things!" Todd's voice was urgent and angry.

"I didn't go through their things. I straightened them. They told you that all was in order. I've done nothing wrong."

There was a pause, then, "Listen to me, Bill Shafer, you need to stay away from those people. I don't hold you responsible for this. But that book is poison—do you hear me? You should have nothing to do with it or them!"

"But . . . no. I'll stay out of the way. It would be embarrassing now if you moved me. I'll stay away." At that point the voices faded as steward and supervisor walked down the hall.

Back in the stateroom, Annie was concerned. "What is it, dear? You've gone pale. And you were very sharp with Mr. Todd."

"The chief steward just berated Bill for looking at the Book of Mormon. He told him it was poison and that he should stay away from us at all costs. He even threatened to transfer him."

"Oh . . ." She sat down heavily.

"I suspected that Todd was anti-Mormon from the look on his face when you handed him the book," Everett added.

"I'm sorry. I saw him put that book in his pocket, and I thought it was the right thing to do. I didn't mean to get him in trouble."

Everett shook his head. "You did nothing wrong. I wish it hadn't happened, since it gives vent to that man's prejudice. But it will be all right." He looked up. "We are who we are, and we have the confidence of knowing that we have the gospel. Whatever problem that man has with us . . . I just hope he doesn't cause too much trouble for the steward." He went over and stood by his dressing chair. "Well, it's over now. I doubt there will be any more issue with it." He started to take his bow tie off and to loosen his cufflinks.

"I wonder why he had a copy of the Book of Mormon," Annie said.

"He tried to hide the cover from me, but when he opened the cover to show me his mother's inscription, he couldn't obscure the copyright."

"Maybe he's a Mormon too."

"That's what I was thinking," said Everett. "Either that, or his mother is. Whatever the answer, he's at risk because of the harsh attitude of his supervisor. If Mr. Todd is as prejudiced as he appears to be, it could cause real problems for Bill."

"What shall we do?"

Everett sat down next to his wife. "Whatever we do, it must be done discreetly. I'd like to find out about Bill, if he'll let us. But we have to be careful so that we don't harm his relationship with his superior any further. At this point I doubt that Todd has realized the book Bill owns is actually the Book of Mormon. He may think Bill's was merely similar. But we must be careful . . ."

Chapter 6

A Disconcerting Mirage

"He's a rotten one, all right. Everybody knows that old John Todd is a pain in the royal rear. You're lucky he didn't fire you on the spot."

"I don't feel lucky, Avery. I don't want to have to face those people again. I didn't do anything wrong, and yet it all blew up in my face."

"You can always work down here. I'd put in a good word for you."

"Work down here—with my body?" To dramatize the sheer absurdity of it, Bill stood up and ran his hands down his slender frame—"slender" being an understatement.

Avery laughed. "Yeah, I guess it would have its problems. And you'd probably choke to death on the coal dust. You always were a frail little thing."

"Not frail. I like to think *lithe.* You never could keep up with me in a race."

"And you could squirm out of nearly any tight spot I put you in. It used to aggravate me no end. It was hard to beat you up properly like an older brother should."

"Sorry I was so difficult. But you see my problem. How do I go back?"

"I wish I knew why Todd was so angry with those people for being Mormon. It's not a crime or anything. I wonder what put the bee under his bonnet."

"Well, at least for the moment, it's working to my advantage, since he seems to be angrier at them than at me."

"Which is why you've got to lie low. All you've got to do is hold out a couple of days, and they'll be off the ship—you'll be home free and clear. Just do what he told you and stay away from them."

"I suppose you're right. Still . . ."

"Ah, so that's it. Even though they treated you like dirt, you like that they're Mormon?"

"Oh, for heaven's sake," Bill sputtered. "They're my passengers, so I'm expected to be interested in them."

"I'm sure that's right," said Avery with a hint of sarcasm.

* * *

EVERETT STOOD LOOKING FORLORNLY OUT to sea as they passed the Irish headlands. In another hour or so, they would break out into the Atlantic, with each nautical mile passed reducing any potential danger from getting wrapped up in some kind of hostility. Still, Everett was subdued, thinking about the incident with the steward.

"It's a lovely sight, don't you think?" Everett jumped as Annie sidled up to him.

"You really would have made a very effective Indian tracker, given your ability to move about noiselessly."

"I startled you?" Annie pretended surprise. It was an old joke between them, and Everett obliged with a laugh.

"Only for the ten thousandth time since we've been married." He took her hand and looked back out to sea. "And yes, it is beautiful. So lush . . . green. I think you'll be surprised by just how dry and desolate Wyoming feels by comparison when you get home."

"At least I'll arrive in time for spring. The shock won't be quite as great."

"I marvel at your optimism, my dear—or is it adaptability?" He was about to say more when there was a disturbance on the other side of the deck. They were on the promenade deck, toward the front of the ship, so it was an easy walk to the other side where a small crowd was gathering.

"There it is again!" someone said urgently.

Everett moved to a spot by the rail. "What's out there? Are dolphins matching our pace?"

"Hardly," the fellow next to him responded. "Someone thought they saw a periscope!"

Everett's stomach lurched.

"Where?"

The supposed witness pointed to a spot slightly behind them on the port side. "I'm pretty sure I saw a glint off the water that could only have been caused by metal."

"Are we in danger?" asked Annie. The mention of the word *periscope* drew others to the railings, and a general sense of alarm rushed through the crowd.

"Will we be sunk?" a woman shouted.

Another repeated Annie's question in a frantic voice. "Are we in danger?"

Everett shook his head and turned to the crowd, raising his voice to make certain that no one started a panic. "We're in no danger now! Rest easy! Even if there were a submarine at that position, it could never catch us. I'm sure the captain is making a good twenty-two knots, and they could never get a good lead on us. If they were out there, they would have fired as we came into range . . . not now."

The fellow they'd been standing next to asked, "And how do you know all this?"

"Basics physics. Even though a torpedo runs slightly faster than the *Lusy,* it could never make up the difference between us and the origin before running out of compressed-air propulsion. Besides, the eyes play tricks on people. A jumping fish. A wave turned back on itself by the wind. Lots of things can cause a reflection on the ocean."

"But it could have been a periscope," the man said defensively.

"Indeed so. Thank heavens the submarine—if any indeed lurk beneath the waves—chose not to fire on us." Everett smiled, given that the number of anxious passengers gathered about him had increased. "If there was a danger, it's passed. Of that I'm certain. And now we'll be moving out of their prowling range." The crowd seemed relieved, but he judged that they could use something else. Turning to the man standing next to him, he said in a strong voice, "I don't know about you, but worrying about such things takes a toll. I think I need some fresh ice cream to calm my nerves. Let's charge it to the Kaiser's account, don't you think?" That did the trick, and the crowd broke up, laughing.

As they made their way inside the ship to the ice cream parlor, Annie leaned close to him and whispered, "You really are rather masterful, my dear. I can sneak up on people, but you can calm them down."

"I really don't think there is any danger. I just don't believe the Germans would attack a passenger liner." He was thoughtful for a moment. "Still, these are uncertain times. I'm beginning to think that the world as we have known it is going to change, and not necessarily for the better."

* * *

BY THEIR THIRD DAY AT sea, it was pretty obvious that Bill Shafer was avoiding them. He'd slip in and do his work when they were out and would sometimes exit the cabin to an adjoining suite when he heard them at their door, as evidenced by the clicking of the side door as they entered.

"I need to talk to him," said Everett.

"Then go down to his pantry. I think he sleeps in a bunk at the back of it, although I'm not sure. The stewards are always just a few steps away."

"A good idea."

Everett started toward the door but was interrupted by Annie. "Why not call him instead?" When she saw his surprised look, she added, "That's what the telephone is for. And he did leave his card."

Everett smiled. "Always the practical one. I've been trying to surprise him in the hall or stumble across him in the cabin, when the answer was right there all along." He picked up the telephone and waited for the crisp, "Ship's operator. How may I help you?"

"I'd like to be connected to our steward, Master Shafer."

"Of course, Mr. Stringham. Just a moment."

"I think I'll go shopping, so the two of you can be alone. I'm the one who embarrassed him, so it would be better if I wasn't here."

A few minutes later, there was a knock on the door. Everett wondered if Bill was as nervous as he was about this.

"Please come in, Bill."

"How may I help you, Mr. Stringham?"

After closing the door, Everett pointed to a chair. "Take a seat. I'd like to ask you a question."

"I'm not really allowed to do that, sir. It would be a violation of protocol."

Everett nodded. "Of course. I understand." He had hoped to sit with Bill but remained standing since the boy refused. "About the other night . . ."

"If there's a problem, sir, I can be assigned to another suite. Mr. Todd thinks that would be better."

Everett shook his head. "There is no problem. And we don't want you replaced. It's just that you had a copy of the Book of Mormon. That's a very unusual thing for someone like me to encounter. My family and I are all members of the LDS Church. While it's probably none of my concern, I would like to understand your circumstance."

Bill started to protest, and his expression became confused. Everett also took a slight step backward to make certain he wasn't coming across as threatening and asked, "Are you a member of the Church? It would be wonderful if you are. I'd like to help you, if I can."

Bill hesitated. "I'm not sure this is appropriate. This is personal and . . ."

"And you're among friends. Even a ship's steward is entitled to a private life."

"Perhaps I will sit down."

"Can I get you something to drink?"

Bill laughed at that. "I'm the one who's supposed to get you a drink, not the other way around."

"In everyday life, perhaps, but in the gospel we're all equal." Everett went over to the bar and poured a glass of water. "Can you tell me about yourself?"

Bill swallowed some of the water and then started his story. "I don't know if I'm a member. My mum joined the church before I was born, something like twenty years ago. Avery was a baby, and my dad wasn't very excited about it. But he loved Mum and wanted her to be happy. She wanted to move to America, but Dad would have none of it, since he was a sailor. So we stayed in Liverpool."

"So you grew up in the Church?"

"I was baptized when I was eight. But there weren't many people in the branch, and my friends at school made fun of me. Avery got in lots of fights over it. When we got older, it became easy to stay away. Now that we both work on the *Lusy,* we never have time to go to church. So it's not much of an issue anymore."

"Your brother works on the *Lusitania*?"

"He's a fireman. He works down in the boiler room. You wouldn't ever think us brothers. He's powerfully built, while I'm rather skinny."

"You look a lot like I did when I was your age."

"Except that you're rich, and I'm just a steward on a passenger liner."

"I was sweeping floors in my father's business when I was your age. So we're really not that different."

The conversation stalled. "About the Book of Mormon . . ."

"Mum gave it to me. She keeps hoping that I'll come back, and it's a comfort to her to think I have the scriptures with me. So I brought the book along. You can imagine how surprised I was when I saw your copy in the nightstand. I'd never seen that book outside of church, so I was just trying to compare it to mine to see if they were the same."

"I'm sorry that my wife misinterpreted what happened. She feels terrible about it."

"It's not her fault. I shouldn't have done it. Still, I meant no harm."

"So what about your father? Is he still outside the Church?"

"Dad died three years ago. Liverpool's a hard town, and he got consumption. It's been miserable for my mother."

Everett allowed the conversation to settle for a moment. "If it's any help, I don't think what you're going through is so uncommon. I didn't know if the Church was true when I was younger. I didn't think about it that much. But I did enjoy my friends at Church and decided that it was a pretty good way to live. I didn't really figure things out until I met Annie and we had our first child. That's when I decided to find out for myself. So I wouldn't worry too much. But I do hope you won't close it out of your life just yet."

"It's not that I'm against the Church. Maybe if we'd had more guys our age, it would be different."

Everett wanted to say more but felt that he'd pushed Bill hard enough already. Just having the conversation meant a lot. "Well, if there's anything I can do . . . For our part, Annie and I are happy to have another member of the Church on the ship with us. If you have any questions, I'd be glad to talk with you about it."

"Thank you." Bill stood up. "I don't mean to be rude, sir, but if I'm away from my duties too long, Mr. Todd is sure to be suspicious."

Everett stood as well. "Why is he so hostile? His reaction the other night quite surprised me."

"I don't know. But he is angry about something. He told me to stay away from you and to avoid anything you have to say to me about religion."

"And yet you came here today."

"I hardly had a choice."

"Sorry about that. I hope I didn't offend you."

"No. Not at all. I liked the American missionaries who used to visit us. I hoped to go to Utah someday. But with the war and all, there's not much chance of that. I've resolved that on my thirty-day leave next month, I'm going to enlist in the navy. My mum doesn't want it, but it's what an Englishman should do."

"Thirty days?"

"Yes, sir. I'm at the end of my contract. When this trip ends with my return to England, I'll be done. When I get home, I'll have a mandatory thirty days' leave before I can sign a new contract with Cunard. But I hope to be enlisted before that."

Everett nodded. "Well, perhaps during your leave you'll think about what I've said. If you ever do decide to come to Utah, you are welcome to stay with us at our Utah home. I know my way around Salt Lake City and would be glad to be your host. In the meantime, maybe you could go to church with your mother during your leave of absence. President Fellowes is a good man, and I'm sure that he'd be glad to see you."

"Perhaps I will, sir. Now, if you'll excuse me."

"Certainly." Everett extended his hand, which Bill took. "No hard feelings?

"No hard feelings."

After the young man had left, Everett sat down and marveled at the conversation.

Chapter 7

When Opportunity Knocks

Everett walked across the room to respond to the knock on the door. It was their fourth day at sea, and they were scheduled to arrive in New York City after dark the next day. They would disembark the following morning. When he opened the door, an older gentleman was standing there.

"May I help you?"

"I hope I can help you, sir. My name is Gliss, Joseph Gliss. I'll be your cabin steward for the remainder of the voyage, and I wanted to see if there was anything I could do for you. I'd be pleased to offer turndown service."

"Our steward? I don't understand. What happened to Bill Shafer?" He paused and then added, "Not that we're not happy to have you with us. I just don't understand why Bill was changed out. It's a bit unusual, isn't it?"

"I can't say, sir. It doesn't happen often, but it does occasionally. At any rate, I don't know why the change was made. I was just assigned to take care of you good people, and so here I am. Do you need ice or drinks?"

Everett attempted a smile. "No, thank you. I think we're fine. Perhaps you could bring us a room service menu. I think I'll order our food in tonight."

"Very good, sir. I'll be back directly."

After closing the door, Everett leaned his back against it with a sigh.

"Mr. Todd must have found out about your visit."

Everett nodded to Annie. "Apparently so. And now young Shafer is paying the price."

"Why do you suppose he is so determined to separate us from the boy?"

"I don't know. He's prejudiced, for some reason. People hear a snippet about the Mormons, and they reject everything about us."

Annie attempted a smile. "Perhaps they just need to know us better . . ."

* * *

"A WORD WITH YOU, MR. TODD! Or should I go to Captain Turner?"

John Todd finally paused and turned around. Everett had been chasing him down the corridor while being completely ignored.

"And how may I help you, Mr. Stringham?"

Everett wanted to hit him rather than talk to him. But that would simply validate the man's prejudice, whatever its cause. "You changed our steward. I want to know why."

"I changed him because the needs of the ship changed. I'm responsible to see that you get good service, and I assigned our most senior steward to your care. Certainly you have nothing to complain about Mr. Gliss? I consider him our best employee."

"No. I have nothing to complain of. He's an outstanding man, just as you say."

"Then it appears we have nothing to talk about. I'll wish you a good day . . ."

"Hold your place, Mr. Todd. For the next twenty-four hours you bear responsibility to hear my complaints, and you will listen to me!"

Todd's face flushed, and he actually stepped toward Everett, as if to strike him. But he caught himself and stepped back. "I apologize. I thought I had heard your concern. You have something else to complain of?"

"I want to know what's happened to Bill Shafer. He did nothing to earn your reproof, and I want to be assured that he's secure in his position. If you've taken punitive action against him because you have some disagreement with me, then I will lodge a complaint against you with the line."

Todd bit his lower lip and scowled. "Mr. Shafer is better off than he was before. I elevated him to serve in the regal suites, which is a great promotion for someone as young as he. So no one can rightly complain of his treatment, particularly Mr. Shafer."

Everett clenched his teeth. "You are a cunning one, aren't you? You have contempt for me, so you pull the boy out of my service in a way that I can make no complaint."

"And how exactly have I displayed contempt for you, sir? Have I said a disparaging word? No. Have I confronted you? No. Instead you assault me and accuse me when I have done nothing but manage my staff. So I will caution you that while a passenger is due every courtesy, I do not have to stand for abuse. Bring your complaints to the captain or whomever else you choose. I have done nothing wrong."

"Why do you hate us? What have we done to you? I saw how you reacted when you found out that we're Mormons. What has happened to make you so vindictive?"

Todd jerked his head involuntarily, and Everett thought Todd really might hit him. In a way he wished he would, because at least then he could work out his anger. "You people . . . your missionaries . . ."

"Yes, what about our missionaries? Have they done something to you?"

Todd shook his head fiercely. "No. I will not be drawn into this. I have done nothing to injure you, and I will not let you provoke me now. But mark my words, Mr. Stringham—you better leave young Shafer alone. If you attempt to talk to him again, I will take action against you. He is not yours to manipulate. Do you understand me?"

"Manipulate? I've never tried to manipulate—"

"DO YOU UNDERSTAND ME, MR. STRINGHAM? LEAVE THE LAD ALONE!"

Everett fell back. He really had no leg to stand on in this dispute. He took a couple of deep breaths to calm himself. "Fine. I have no idea what's happened to you, but I am sorry that it did. Thank you for talking with me. I won't have occasion to speak with you again."

To his surprise, Todd let him have the final word, as evidenced by the fact that he quickly turned and walked away without saying another word. Everett let out a sigh and returned to his cabin, where he went in and told Annie everything that had transpired. Unfortunately, she was not sympathetic. "Sometimes it's best to let things lie, Everett. You had your chance to talk to Bill Shafer, and perhaps he'll go to church again. As for Mr. Todd, he is within his rights. I'm surprised you would confront him."

"Et tu, Brute?"

Annie softened but didn't yield. "It's not your fight, dear. You've taken what should have been a magnificent voyage home on this wonderful ship and have muddied the experience by stewing about this. People are prejudiced—that's not new. Bill Shafer isn't a faithful member of the Church—that's his business. I will be leaving you in a few days. I'd like to spend them with the usually happy, pleasant man that I love. Can't you let this go?"

Everett sank down into the chair. When he spoke, his voice was tight with emotion. "It's just that it matters to me. I want Bill Shafer to feel differently about things. I want him to see what he's missing . . ."

"Bill Shafer or Leonard?"

"Leonard? What's he got to do with this?"

"He's your son. And he's no longer participating in church. You feel guilty for that, even though you shouldn't. Now you find this young man whom you'd like to rescue. I can't help but believe it's all tied together somehow."

Everett stood up abruptly. "I need a walk."

"Everett, I'm sorry. I didn't mean to upset you more."

"It's all right. You're probably right. But I can't make sense of it all right now. I need to go for a walk and think." He softened. "I just need some fresh air. It'll help me cheer up."

"I hope so." Annie accepted a light kiss on her cheek, although it was evident that she was still perplexed. Everett stepped out the door.

Half an hour or so later, he found himself down on the lower decks of the ship. He'd walked back and forth the full length of the ship, passing rather than exploring each of the decks in turn. Now he was at a dead end, where the only way forward was through a door marked CREW ONLY. He knew he should go back, but he couldn't. So he simply slumped down onto the linoleum floor with his head in his hands. He may even have fallen asleep. At least he was unaware of the time when a voice broke into his reverie.

"Can I help you, sir? Have you lost your way?"

He looked up into the face of a heavily built young man. Everett was quite certain he'd seen him before.

"Can I help you? You really shouldn't be down here. It's not safe for passengers."

This was perhaps the first time that Everett noticed how loud the sounds of mechanical equipment were and realized he must be near the boiler rooms. When the young man persisted, Everett finally allowed the lad to extend a hand to help him stand up. "I'm fine. I think I can find my way back to the proper deck."

"I'm happy to show you the way."

"Thank you, but I'm sure I can find my way." He paused for a moment. "Have we met before?"

"Not that I know of. We never get passengers down in this part of the ship, and I don't make it up top."

"That's strange—I'm sure I've seen you before." Everett shrugged. "Oh, well, I guess not. Thank you for your help." Then he noticed the name on the young man's uniform. "Shafer? Is that your name?"

"Yes, sir. Avery Shafer."

"You're Bill Shafer's brother—the fireman."

"Yes, sir. He's my brother. So Bill is your steward, then?" Avery seemed relieved to figure out their connection.

"Was my steward. Then John Todd intervened."

"Oh, so you're the folks who got Bill in trouble. The Mormons from Wyoming."

"The very same. I'm afraid I've made a mess of things for your brother . . . although he seems to have gotten a promotion out of it."

Avery nodded. "John Todd's a blaggard. But he is in control. I've told Bill to leave well enough alone."

"Probably good advice, but it's very unsatisfying that I can't talk to whom I choose." He tried to force a smile. "We Americans aren't used to being restricted, you know?"

"I do know that. I noticed that quality in all the missionaries who paraded through our house. My mum loves them. If she had her way, we'd go on missions."

"Well, I should try to talk you into it as well, but my wife says I meddle too much. So I think I'll take a pass. That is, unless you want a promotion too? Perhaps talking to me will be as good for your career as it was for Bill's."

Avery laughed. "I think I'm fine where I'm at. Bill is very sorry that he got transferred away. He actually liked you and your wife. The way I see it, you were just doing what you felt was right, as a church member."

"Church! That's where I saw you—at the branch in Liverpool. I hadn't made the association before. But you attended church, didn't you?"

Avery's face reddened. "Yes, sir. Perhaps that's it, although I don't recall seeing you. My mum wanted me to go."

"You were there with a young lady, if I remember right." He thought for a moment. "And a child?"

Avery took a moment to clear his throat, clearly embarrassed by this. "She's a widow. Mum invited her to our church, and she accepted. I think it was my mother's way of getting me there."

"Bill explained that you and he aren't really active in the Church."

"Yes, well, Mary seemed to enjoy it." Then Avery fell silent, obviously uncomfortable at this turn in the conversation.

"Well, thanks, I've been rather miserable since all this happened with Bill. But there's nothing to be done about it. Please tell Bill that I hope we didn't cause him too much trouble. I wish I had a chance to spend more time with him. I see a lot of potential in him."

"That's Bill. Actually, I wish you had more time with him as well. He misses our father and has never quite figured things out since then. Too bad that voyages come to an end and that blokes like Todd stick their noses into other people's business."

Everett turned to walk away, but after three or four steps he hesitated and stopped. Turning, he said, "Say, Avery. Can you tell me what you crew members do while you're in New York? Do you have to stay with the ship, or do you get to go into the city?"

"It depends. I have to stay and do maintenance on the boilers during this turnaround—it's a way to earn a little extra money. But Bill is on his own. He'll probably go to a cheap hotel with some of the others and go watch a boxing match or something."

"Could you get a message to Bill?"

"Sure."

"I just had a thought. It may be a bit daft, but perhaps I could tell you what I'm thinking and you tell me if you think I'm crazy."

"Oh, I think it's too late for that, sir. John Todd's been hinting at that all along."

Everett laughed. "He's not worth the trouble of proving wrong, is he?"

"Nah. Todd's a real blighter. Everyone knows that. You don't need to worry on his account. People probably think more highly of you because he doesn't like you. Now what's this idea you have for Bill?"

Everett stepped forward and started telling him his plan. At first Avery shook his head but eventually changed it into a nod. "It might work. I'll ask him. It's a bit out of character for him, but it would probably be good for him. At the very least it would give Mum a thrill."

"I hope so. Tell him I'm very serious. I'd enjoy his company."

Chapter 8
Very Different Agendas

"This fog is maddening," said Weisig. "Not only does it blind us, but it muffles the sound and confuses direction. Even if we were to hear something, I'm not sure we could discern its direction."

"Perhaps we should submerge and wait for the fog to lift," replied First Officer Braun.

"What? With the batteries only half charged! Don't be a fool." Weisig immediately regretted his choice of words, since Lieutenant Braun often brooded at a perceived insult. "I didn't mean that, Braun—at least not the way it sounded. What I wanted to say is that we need to stay on the surface and charge the batteries."

"Yes, sir. Of course. I'll ensure the lookouts are particularly vigilant." If Braun was wounded, his voice didn't betray it.

They had been at sea for nearly ten days with only one small merchantman to show for their efforts. Their belly was full of torpedoes, and the crew was restless. In a noticeably flat voice, Weisig said, "Schweiger will be setting sail tomorrow. With his luck, the days will be clear and fair."

A slight smile creased Braun's lips. Weisig liked to pretend he wasn't competitive, but then something like this would slip out, showing just how desperately he wanted to better the captain of *U-20.* "You've been out here a long time, Captain. Perhaps you should go below. I'll call you if we hear anything."

Weisig straightened his back and clapped his gloved hands together a couple of times as if to warm them. "No, I want to stay here awhile. I need the fresh air. But I would appreciate it if you would go below and talk with Heinze about engine number three. It doesn't sound right to me, and I'd like to know what he intends to do for it. Just in case we get the chance to pursue."

"Of course. I'll see to it immediately." Braun saluted and then descended the ladder into the control room, where he worked his way aft to the engine room. On the way, he encountered a veritable obstacle course: stepping over crates of stored food as he passed through the galley, avoiding the men who were sleeping in their shared hammocks, saluting the officers in the wardroom who stood up abruptly from their card game until he finally passed through the watertight bulkhead and into the engine room. The noise was overwhelming from the sound of two of the four diesels pounding furiously away to charge the batteries. The normal procedure when surfaced was to use two diesels to charge the batteries and two to provide directional thrust. If they had to move quickly, all four diesels could be used for propulsion. But with the heavy fog, the captain had ordered the ship to sustain just enough power to maintain trim, so one engine was off, the other idling. Still, the two functioning engines were loud enough to make conversation difficult, to say the least.

Motioning at the chief engineer, Braun shouted, "The captain thinks engine three is making unnatural sounds and wants to know what you plan to do about it!"

Chief Heinze said, "I've got two men working on it. We think it's a bearing but haven't determined that for certain. That's why I'm running it under stress. Once we know, we'll take it offline and use engine one for charging."

"If it is a bearing, how long will it take to repair?" Braun hated yelling, but it was the only way to be heard. Heinze motioned for him to step through the bulkhead.

They couldn't close the door because the engines were drawing so much air that it was providing additional circulation inside the boat—a real benefit for the men who normally had to endure stale, hot air. But they stepped to the side of the doorway where the metal wall separated them from much of the engine noise. "I'm not sure we can repair it," said Heinze in a quieter voice.

"What do you mean? We can't operate on three engines! The captain could require full speed at any time!"

"Yes, sir," said Heinze stiffly. "I'm aware of that." But he didn't offer any consolation or alternative.

Braun bit his lip. "So at this point you don't know the problem for sure; the engine has an unusual sound but is working effectively. If there was an emergency, we could count on it coming online—is that a fair assessment?"

"Not exactly. The engine is running very hot. I will have to take it offline in the next five minutes, regardless of whether we've fully identified the cause. We'll then go to work to see if it can be repaired. If it is the bearing that I think it is, however, we don't have a replacement on board, nor can we fabricate one. In that case, the engine will have to be taken out of service."

"Except in an emergency—you could use it in an emergency . . ."

Heinze inhaled sharply at Braun's apparent inability to understand what he was saying. This was the sort of thing the captain would understand instantly, which is why Heinze and many others harbored doubts about Braun's ability to provide leadership should something happen to the captain. Doing his best to steady his voice, Heinze replied, "If it is a bearing, the engine will overheat with even minor use. It could very easily start a fire. My professional advice would be that you not use the engine even in an emergency. But you are the officers, and my men and I will do as you tell us." He caught himself before adding, "Even though we'd be the ones to get burned to death if you did."

Apparently that was clear enough even for Braun, who simply shrugged his shoulders. "Well, then, as you were. I'll report to the captain."

Making his way forward, he didn't take as much care as he passed the various obstacles in his way. This news of the engine was very demoralizing, although certainly not fatal to their mission. He just regretted that it was he who would have to tell the captain. Weisig would not be pleased.

Unfortunately, what had been a theoretical mental exercise just a few moments earlier became reality as Braun was about to ascend up the ladder. The telegraph sounded shrilly as the order came from the bridge to come to full speed. That meant all four engines—except for the uncertainty of the flawed bearing.

“What rotten timing,” said Braun as he flew up the ladder. “And I’m the one who has to report our condition to the captain. I just hope we’re the attacker, not the defender!” Of course that was a foolish thing to say since the captain would have ordered a dive if they were under attack. Clearly there was a prize out there, and Weisig would be furious if engine three had to be shut down. It was an ill omen no matter how one thought about it.

* * *

New York City

“WE MISSED SEEING THE STATUE of Liberty.”

“Another disappointment. Sorry.”

Annie shrugged. “It’s all right. I’m glad to be here. It wasn’t such a fun voyage.”

“I’m sorry about that, too,” said Everett. “It’s my fault.”

“It’s all right. You were provoked.”

Everett and Annie were standing at the railing for one last look at the New York skyline from the deck of the *Lusitania*. They would be called to disembark shortly.

“Everett, Sir William is motioning for you.”

“What?” Everett turned and saw his British friend some distance off. “I wonder what this is all about.”

“You’d better go see. He’s rather a formidable fellow.”

He nodded and moved down the railing. “Sir William?”

“Ah, yes—Stringham. Thank you for coming over.”

“How can I help you?”

“I just wanted to say I enjoyed your company. You’re a very genial fellow and are well informed on a variety of subjects. If you’re ever in London, you should look me up. I’d be glad to take you to my club. It can be a respite from the noise of the city.”

“I’d like that. In fact, I will be there in a couple of weeks, so I just may take you up on it.” Everett smiled. “And to reciprocate your generous invitation, please visit me the next time you’re in Wyoming.” Sir William was a bit flustered until Everett broke into a grin and laughed.

“Yes, well—perhaps I will surprise you and actually come there someday. All your talk about Yellowstone Park and the excellent big-game hunting has intrigued me. Maybe after this infernal war is over, we can find time."

"Well, you're certainly welcome, and we will see to it that you are well cared for." The two men shook hands, and Everett returned to join Annie.

"Do you think he'll meet us?" It took a moment to register that she was not talking about Sir William.

"I hope so. Of course, I couldn't talk to him without making things worse." Everett cast a sideways glance at Annie. "And as my lovely wife explained to me so well, there are times when it's better to let things sort themselves out."

"It's about time you believed me."

"It looks as if Mr. Gliss is waving at us." Everett turned, and, sure enough, their steward was motioning for them to come to the bulkhead door.

"Pardon me, sir. But it's time for your disembarkation. Your bags have all been taken to the pier by the porters, and I understand that a carriage is waiting for you."

"Thank you, Gliss. You've offered superb service. It was a pleasure to be in your care."

"Thank you, sir, for choosing Cunard. There's no finer ship in the world than the *Lusy,* as far as I'm concerned. And you and Mrs. Stringham have been very kind to me."

Everett handed him a generous tip. With that, the Stringhams made their way to the first-class elevators and down to the gangplank.

As they made their way through customs, Everett kept glancing over his shoulder but saw nothing. Finally, they made their way to the curb, where a horse-drawn carriage was waiting. There were a few motorized cabs on the streets, but most people preferred the quieter gait of a horse.

"It looks like he isn't coming," said Annie.

"We'll give him a few more minutes. It's possible he got held up in leaving the ship."

Finally, just as they were about to give up, Annie pointed. "Look, there he is!" Sure enough, Bill Shafer came ambling toward them, a duffel bag in his hand.

Everett broke loose and jogged over to him. "So you got my message from Avery?"

Bill smiled nervously. "He told me I'd be a fool not to take you up on this. But I feel like I'm imposing. I've never done anything like this in my life."

Everett looked as if a great weight had been lifted from his chest, and Annie smiled to see her husband so happy. "I'm very glad that you've decided to join us, Bill. I hope you won't feel awkward about it. All that first-class malarkey really isn't who we are."

"I'm sorry we got crossed up. But you're sure it's all right? I'm more than able to take care of myself in New York City."

"Of course you are. But it isn't often that we get a chance to spend a few days with a friend. You'll be back on the ship in plenty of time."

"I've never had a chance like this." Out of his steward uniform he looked much more like the boy he really was. And the excitement he displayed was infectious.

"So what do I need to do?"

"Just put your bag in the back of the carriage, and we'll be off to the Waldorf-Astoria. To my reckoning, it's the finest hotel in New York City."

"So much for our protestations that we're not first-class sort of people. We hardly need the Waldorf."

Everett blushed at Annie's reproof. "The reservations were already made. I know it's foolish, but . . ."

"Yes, I know, but business has been good." Annie turned to Bill. "He's got a good heart. And you will be our guest, not a servant. So please relax and enjoy."

"I'll try, ma'am."

"Let's get going, then."

But before Bill got his bag to the coachman, John Todd burst out of nowhere. "So you ARE going with them! I told you to stay away from these people."

Everett wheeled around. "What are you doing here?"

"I'm rescuing my young charge from you, you blighter!"

"How dare you. You know perfectly well that Mr. Shafer has the weekend off, and he is beyond your reach or Cunard's. Everyone is entitled to their personal affairs, and Bill has chosen to spend his time with us. It's nothing more complicated than that, and it's really none of your business, anyway."

"What is it, Bill? Are you going to believe me or these . . . these Mormons?"

Bill's face was ashen. "I don't . . . I don't know . . ."

"Listen to me, Todd. I've put up with your insolence enough. Whatever you have against me, let's have it out. Obviously you hate me for my religion—but that's not enough to justify this harassment. If there's something I've done, tell me. If there's some reason you don't trust me, then make it known. But do not make recriminations on this young man, and do not impugn my wife. I will not stand for it!"

By this point, the driver of the cab had come around, and he was a formidable fellow. "Is this man giving you trouble, sir? I'd be glad to handle it, if you like."

At exactly the same moment, Everett spied something that added to his confidence—a bowler hat. "Perhaps we should invite Captain Turner over to see how you treat your first-class passengers." He motioned in the direction of Will Turner. "In fact, I think that's exactly what we should do."

As Everett started toward the captain, who was walking confidently down the street by himself, John Todd put out his hand and stopped him. "No! We don't need to disturb the captain. He likes his privacy."

"Then will you stop accosting us? And will you promise that you'll allow Bill back on the ship on good terms when he returns?"

"May I ask where you're taking him?"

"No, you may not. But he will be safe, and he will be in a moral and upright environment. Certainly you can appreciate that."

Todd scowled. "I have my doubts about that. But since I must yield, I'll leave you now." Todd turned to Bill. "You can come back to the ship—you're a good worker. But you're a fool to listen to what this man has to say. A fool who has much to lose, I promise you that." To emphasize his point, John Todd spat on the ground—not directly at Everett, but close enough to show his contempt. Then he wheeled around and disappeared as quickly as he had come.

As Todd disappeared around a corner, Everett felt himself shaking, he was so angry. He opened and closed his hands until his heart slowed a little. Gaining control, he finally said, "I'm sorry about that, Bill. I have no idea why he harbors such animosity."

"I think you were amazing. No one stands up to John Todd like that. He deserved it."

"It's not something I like doing, but I'll certainly stand up and fight for my family."

"Well it was very distasteful," said Annie. "I'm glad it's settled. Can we be off now? I want to be done with all this." Annie had spoken, and so it was. They stepped up into the cab, and before long Everett was chatting cheerfully as he pointed out the sites of what he considered one of the greatest cities of the world.

Chapter 9

New York City and Action Off the Irish Coast

"So tell me again who it is we're going to meet?" After settling in at the Waldorf-Astoria at Thirty-Fifth Street and Fifth Avenue, Bill had joined the Stringhams for lunch in the hotel restaurant.

"It's my cousin and her husband," replied Annie.

"And why is he famous?"

Annie cast something of an annoyed glance at Everett. "He is not famous. He's one of the General Authorities of our church. He's coming through New York City after a trip to Boston and other cities in New England to hold church conferences. I'm leaving Manhattan with them tomorrow so he can speak at a conference in Ohio on Sunday. That's all."

Bill nodded. "My mum would think he's famous. She always made us go to church when a General Authority was coming through Liverpool. I liked to hear them speak."

"If you're up to it, we'd like to go touring the city this afternoon, and then we'll meet them at the train station at five o'clock. Then it's off to a Yankees game for the men and to a poetry reading for the ladies. They're being hosted by one of the members of the Church here in New York City. Men aren't invited, apparently."

"We're only going there because you and Henry didn't want to go to the opera. I still think we should all go to the opera instead," said Annie with a sniff. "It would be good for you."

Everett bit his lower lip to suppress a smile. "I'm sure it would, my dear, but Bill here has never been to a baseball game, and you have to agree that there's nothing more American than baseball."

"Can a General Authority go to a baseball game? I thought they had to wear a suit all the time and do religious things."

"Elder Carlson probably will wear a suit," said Everett. "Of course, we'll wear sport jackets to be properly attired; we'll stop and get one for you if you don't have one."

"I have a jacket—Cunard expects us to dress well while we're going about the city."

"Good. At any rate, Elder Carlson will be dressed properly. But *Hank* Carlson is a huge baseball fan and a terrific baseball player in his own right. He was a famous pitcher for the University of Utah before he became a lawyer." This time he did not yield to Annie. "He *was* famous, dear. A local hero for all the boys who dream of growing up to be a baseball player."

"A General Authority *plays* baseball?" Now Bill was incredulous.

"They're only men," replied Annie. "Very good men who have important work to do. But they are called to service from out of the ranks of the Church. It isn't like other churches where a man goes to college to become a paid minister or priest. All our leaders grew up just like you."

Bill looked dubious, so Annie added, "There's nothing to say that you won't be called to some important church position some day."

"That's not likely. At least until I start going to church more often."

"I'm sorry we can't hear Elder Carlson speak this weekend," said Everett. It was always a little difficult knowing what to call Carlson: Elder or Henry or Hank. "He really is a good man, and I think you'd enjoy hearing what he has to say. But Annie and the Carlsons leave on Friday, and the ship sails on Saturday, so we don't have much time together. But at least we get to spend time with him tonight and tomorrow, so you'll get to know him."

"And you can ask him any questions you might have," added Annie. "He has a son about your age, so you shouldn't feel intimidated."

"It is kind of different—spending time with you, meeting a General Authority, going to a baseball game." Bill shook his head. "I'd never dreamed anything like this could happen."

Everett was immensely pleased. "Well, we're going to have a splendid day together seeing the sites. Then off to the Polo Grounds to see the Yankees play tonight. Tomorrow we'll go to some art galleries in the morning before we see Annie off." He turned and smiled at Annie. "Penance for our baseball game."

Annie shook her head. "Everett . . ."

"I'm kidding. Actually, I want to buy a painting for Annie to memorialize our trip together. We don't get to travel all that often, and I want something beautiful to hang in our parlor that will remind us of our time in England and New York."

Bill nodded, apparently satisfied that going with them was the right thing to do.

"You can stay at the hotel and relax, if you like," Everett added.

"No, I'd like to go with you, if you don't mind. Since working on the *Lusitania,* I've learned to like looking at the paintings. I think it would be interesting."

"Good," said Annie. "Then there's something interesting for all of us to do." She smiled at Everett. "I'm glad you invited Bill to come along. It's making the day much more fun."

"Well, then, let's get going! Time is wasting."

* * *

"What is it, Captain—do we have a target?" Braun was breathless as he reached the bridge.

Weisig pointed to starboard. "There—through that break in the fog. Do you see it?"

Braun peered through his binoculars then smiled. "I do indeed." But as he stared a bit longer, the smile faded, "It's a British lightship, if I'm not mistaken." He was about to add, "Certainly you won't attack that . . ." but Weisig started talking first.

"Do you realize what we can do to coastal shipping by sinking that ship? It will be chaos all through this channel, with ships having to pass farther out to sea to avoid the rocks. Their exposure to our submarines will be terrific, at least until the lightship can be replaced. But of course that could take months—maybe even a year."

"But a lightship . . ."

Weisig turned on Braun, reacting to the tone in his voice. "Yes, Mr. Braun, a lightship. A movable lighthouse—a vessel created to warn ships at sea of hazards, bellowing its foghorn on days like this and shining its electric light from the masthead at night. A perfect aid to the people who are our enemies." By now his face was rock hard. "I can't imagine that you have any objection to that . . ."

Braun inhaled deeply. "Of course not. It is fortuitous that we came upon it."

"It's fortuitous that we didn't run into the rocks ourselves," said Weisig, the excitement returning to his voice. He raised his binoculars again and studied the scene.

"Make ready a challenge!" he called down to the gun crew. "We've got to be quick about it." They had to be quick enough to get the crew off the lightship before a wireless was sent out calling for help. That would be the best outcome, since it would leave ships traveling in the area completely oblivious to their danger, hopefully leading to a number of shipwrecks. Next best would be that if a wireless was sent that the lightship had been sunk, the ships at sea would become disoriented and fearful, which would serve Germany's purpose nearly as well—with shipping in the area becoming tied up and inefficient. The worst outcome would be for Weisig and his crew to take so long attempting to sink the lightship that the British could dispatch a warship to save it. Weisig was not about to let that happen.

"Ready to shoot!" came a shout from the deck.

"Good. Any moment now . . ." replied Weisig. Then he hesitated. "Why aren't we at full speed? I'm quite certain I ordered full speed ahead."

"You did, Captain. It's number three. A bad bearing. The Chief had to shut it down or risk a fire . . ." Braun's voice trailed off miserably as he saw the look that news momentarily put on Weisig's face.

But to his surprise, Weisig simply bit his lip and said, "We'll get by on three engines, then." As they came into sight of the lightship, they saw one of the men on the enemy ship suddenly notice them, prompting a flurry of activity. But there really was nothing the poor little ship could do, since it was tethered to a huge mushroom anchor that trailed far out to sea to hold the ship in place in even the fiercest of gales. It took a lightship several hours to recover the anchor in the best of conditions, and this ship had less than half of an hour to live.

"Shoot!" shouted Weisig. The deck gun crackled instantly to life, the fiery blast from its muzzle lighting up the now-fading fog. The shell passed harmlessly across the deck of the lightship, as was intended, and within a matter of moments the captain of the vessel came out on deck waving a white flag.

"SOS signal being sent out!" came an urgent message through the voice tube. Weisig's radio operator had, of course, been monitoring the situation.

"I guess you can't fault them for that," said Weisig. "Signal them to abandon ship and to be quick about it. We don't have time to be idle." There was genuine concern in his voice, since this was a busy shipping lane and it was quite likely that other ships were in the vicinity—ships that could be potential targets, or perhaps British warships that would move immediately against them.

"I doubt a lightship has ever been sunk in battle before," said Braun quietly. He maintained his tone of voice in such a way that his comment could be interpreted as a compliment, even though that was definitely not the intention. While he shared the captain's enthusiasm for the effect it would have on hostile shipping, he also realized that many neutral ships and noncombatants passed this way, and they would now all be placed in peril.

"Well, it's about to happen for the first time, then," replied Weisig in a strained voice. He was quiet for a few moments, the brow of his forehead furrowed in deep concentration. Then, with a steely look in his eyes, he turned to Braun, "And you shall have the honor of being the one to give the order, Mr. Braun."

"What? But it is your kill. You spotted it . . ." Braun hated the fact that he was stammering, even as he struggled to get the words out.

"No less credit to me if you execute the order." Weisig straightened up and announced to the bridge crew, "I'm going below. Mr. Braun will conduct the attack. I want that ship on the bottom of the ocean within the hour." Turning to Braun, he added, "Give those men no more than ten minutes to abandon ship. Then shoot below the waterline. I don't want any time wasted, or any torpedoes for that matter." Speaking more loudly so that everyone on the deck crew could hear him, he added, "This is a great day for Germany." He then stiffened and saluted the crew, all of whom quickly responded in kind.

"Make it fast, Mr. Braun. And make it deadly!"

"Sir!" Braun's hand was trembling as he brought it to the visor of his cap—whether from anger or fear, Weisig didn't care. It was time for his first officer to live up to his responsibility.

* * *

SITTING AT THE TINY DESK in his cabin, Weisig felt the boat shudder as the deck gun fired round after round of ammunition. He could easily picture the effect on the lightship—the first rounds would strike below the waterline to start the ship sinking. Next would be one or two shells to topple the mast that supported the warning light—not really necessary, but providing great satisfaction for the crew. And it did serve a purpose of sorts in that if they had to break away from the encounter before the lightship was fully submerged, they would at least know that the ship's main function was destroyed.

He sighed as the deck guns fell silent. That meant the deed was done. The crew of the lightship would be dejectedly rowing to shore while Lieutenant Braun brooded, doing his best to appear manly about the whole thing. The crew would be rejoicing. The torpedo men would be a little subdued because it was the gun crew who earned the honor of the kill, but that was of little concern. They still had plenty of time to find even worthier targets. He thought for a moment about going up on deck but decided that this was Braun's moment. So he started writing about the incident in his official log. Braun would be down shortly to fill in the details.

Perhaps five minutes later, he must have been lost in concentration, because the sound of the diving alarm nearly scared him out of his wits. The pencil fell to the floor as Weisig lurched out of his chair toward the conning tower, suppressing the urge to shout out for an update. Then he heard the fateful sound that answered the question before it was even asked. "We'll never make it," he mumbled to himself, since he didn't want the crew to hear the terror in his voice. He reached the bottom of the ladder just as Braun came crashing down it, pulling the hatch closed behind him. Weisig let him report, even though he knew perfectly well what was happening.

"British destroyer bearing down on us. They're going to ram!" The fear in Braun's voice—in fact, in the whole control room—was palpable.

"Emergency dive—flood everything!" said Weisig. But the sound of the enemy propeller was simply too loud. The only question now was where the blow would fall. "Everyone brace for collision! Prepare to abandon ship!" These orders were expected of him, but for most of the crew it was hopeless. The submarine would be like a giant coffin for them, with no way out before the water came in. As the sound of the propeller neared, they felt their ship start to tremble from the forward wash of the bow of the destroyer. Weisig glanced around the room, knowing that in a moment or two, most of these men would be dead. The radio operator had tears on his face, but he was brave enough not to say anything. The planesman was leaning on the dive planes with all his weight, but the little boat simply couldn't dive fast enough for it to make a difference. In fact it would undoubtedly make the situation much worse that they were flooding the ballast tanks, since the ship would continue sinking after the collision, rather than bobbing to the surface as it might if they still had buoyancy in the tanks.

Leaning close to Braun, Weisig whispered, "Justice and retribution, I suppose, for killing a lightship." Everyone in the world knew that lightships had a special place in sailors' hearts, since they were the boats that saved people's lives. It really was an act of desecration—what they had done—almost equal on a scale of evil to firing on a hospital ship.

"Oh, Captain," said Braun miserably. "I did my duty . . . you can't . . ."

"Forget it!" shouted Weisig. It was difficult to make himself heard now. "We all did our duty, and now we will pay the price for it!"

And then the price came due. Just when he thought the noise couldn't get any louder, there was a violent impact as the destroyer crashed into the conning tower, accompanied by the incredible sound of tearing, crashing, and rending of metal. The force of the collision was so great that the submarine started to roll to its side. The impact was so powerful that virtually all the men were thrown violently against the panels and controls with such incredible force that one man screamed out in agony—his side punctured by an exposed handle. The shock was so terrific, in fact, that Weisig saw the figurative stars in his eyes, the impact on his optic nerve creating false images of light.

Once the destroyer had passed over them, the ship settled slightly, and Weisig shook his head to clear it. "Everyone make your way out of the ship whatever way you can," he shouted. No one heard him, of course, because the commotion of the ship literally being turned turtle in the water still made coherent thoughts impossible. Still, Weisig was surprised that more water hadn't flooded in—and then he realized that despite the initial blow's having torn a gash right through the conning tower, the speed of the destroyer was such that it had flipped them completely upside down so that the water would shortly be coming up around their legs, rather than raining down on them from above. In one of those ironies of submarines, it would actually be more difficult for water to come in with the boat topsy-turvy, since the compressed air inside the boat would have no natural way to escape with the hatches facing down into the water. But it would be a temporary reprieve at best.

As he tried to struggle to his feet, Weisig was appalled to find himself stepping on one of his crew. The man cried out in pain, and Weisig quickly bent down to help him, but his face was a bloody, unrecognizable mess, undoubtedly smashed against some protrusion as the ship tumbled. Weisig recoiled from the sight and decided not to do anything, since there was no way to comfort him. The sound of men screaming and thrashing throughout the ship was more than he could take, and he heard himself crying out in despair.

"There's still hope," he said desperately. Men had escaped from rammed submarines before. But perhaps not from an incident like this. He looked around and saw Braun crumpled at his side, either knocked dead or unconscious. If he didn't regain consciousness quickly, he would certainly die.

"Abandon ship!" Weisig shouted. It startled some men enough that they started making their way toward the emergency hatches, but before they could make real progress, a torrent of water came cascading in on them with such force that no one could make their way against the current. As he watched one after the other thrown back by the onrushing water, he concluded that one or more of the torpedo tubes must have ruptured from the pressure, which meant that the air inside the boat now had a way to escape. Seawater would come in just as fast as the air evacuated. As the freezing water started up Weisig's legs, he felt the warmth of tears on his own face. This was his command, and he had failed it. When the lights went out a moment later, he knew that they would all die in darkness. "The war is over for us," Captain Weisig cried quietly to the darkness.

They were the last words he spoke before being quickly submerged in water with no place to go. He had just thirty seconds to hold his breath—perhaps a few seconds more—and then he would have to yield to the involuntary response to open his mouth to gasp for air. It would take only a few moments after that and his consciousness would fade away, his life at an end.

* * *

New York

"THEY'VE DONE IT AGAIN," said Everett with disgust, shaking his head at the newspaper he was reading over breakfast.

"Done what, dear?"

Everett folded the paper and set it to the side. "The Germans have sunk to a new low, as far as I'm concerned. They attacked and sank a British lightship. It seems they're deadly serious about this unrestricted warfare doctrine of theirs."

Annie looked up. They were both enjoying a late breakfast after the late ending of the Yankees game, which had gone to two extra innings. Bill was still asleep, or so they assumed, since there was no noise coming from the room adjoining their suite. So rather than wait, they had ordered room service.

"At least they sank the German submarine," said Everett as he read farther in the article. "They rammed it, and the thing went down with all hands lost."

Annie reacted to the satisfaction in his voice. "Everett, that isn't something to rejoice over. Those men were just serving their government. I'm sure there are dozens of bereaved families back in Germany."

"Yes, but to attack a lightship—who can say what is next on their list of terrible deeds?"

"Which is why I wish you'd just come home with us. I'm sure you can get those contracts signed by mail. I don't like the idea of your going back and forth across the ocean in such dangerous times."

Everett's eyes widened as the conversation took this unexpected turn. He'd hoped to avoid this type of discussion, and now he'd brought it on. "It's more than just getting some documents signed—I need to complete the negotiations. We want to be sensitive to the dire circumstances of the British government and yet protect the interests of our owners. I really need to be there."

Annie sighed but didn't say anything. Everett felt uncomfortable but didn't know what to do about it. On the one hand, it was foolish for him to travel so extensively during a time of war—Annie was right about that. Yet he had accepted the position within the association and felt duty-bound to carry out his responsibilities. It wasn't exactly a point of conflict between them, but it was sensitive.

Everett read in silence for a while, not sure how to continue the conversation. Annie took him off the spot, however. "So how did Henry and Bill get along?"

"Splendidly. Hank absolutely charmed him. They'd talk cricket one moment, then baseball, and then in an almost magical fashion Hank would weave something in about the Church—talking about an all-church tournament he'd played in, or something like that. Before you knew it, he'd extracted a promise from Bill to come to Salt Lake City when the war is over, and he promised to look Bill up when he was in England. He really is good with youths."

"I think that's why he was called to serve."

"Well, I couldn't have been happier. I'd like to think we could make a difference in this young man's life—even though I know a few days together can't really change him."

"You'll have time with him when you're in Liverpool. Who knows where this will lead?"

Everett nodded contentedly. Annie's comment about Liverpool told him that she'd forgiven him for going back to England.

"Could I have a bit more of that orange juice?" he asked.

ıAPTER 12

ɲ ˎ JUDGE A MAN

Apr' –Wilhelmshaven, Germany

" ," SAID WALTHER SCHWEIGER, captain of *U-20,* "you ¸ot yourself killed. So much for our bet." He stood looking his submarine, about to set sail into the very same waters .d become the final resting place of Weisig and his crew. "Pe. aps I'll get a kill for you—revenge is an honorable way to salute a fallen comrade."

"Pardon me, Captain, but you asked me to report when all is ready."

Schweiger turned and acknowledged the salute of his first officer. "Very good. Please muster the crew, and I will come aboard."

"Yes, sir. May I ask our destination?"

Schweiger shook his head. "There are no special orders. We've been given general instructions, but it's really up to us."

"Have you decided where to concentrate?"

"St. George's Channel, I think. With the British disaster that is unfolding at Gallipoli in the eastern Mediterranean, we've heard that three of Cunard's and White Star's best ships are being pressed into service as troop transports: *Olympic, Aquitania,* and *Mauretania.* Wouldn't that be something to sink one of those nameplates? British arrogance would be severely tarnished by that."

"Yes, sir." The man smiled but then became serious. "They're still very fast."

Schweiger nodded. "But there are three of them! The odds are in our favor."

* * *

April 30, 1915—New York City

EVERETT WAS SUBDUED. HE FELT depressed at the thought of having put Annie on the train earlier that afternoon. While he was excited to return to England, he was already lonesome without her. Now he was out for a walk alone, after having a quiet dinner with Bill.

Bill had expressed concern about Everett walking alone at night, but he promised to stay close to the hotel, and Bill had said he'd catch up with Everett in a few minutes after he went up to his room.

New York was unseasonably warm on this last night of April, so he left his coat unbuttoned. The *Lusitania* was to depart from Pier 54 the next morning, so after separating from Annie, Everett had moved himself and Bill to the Excelsior for their last night in town, a hotel much closer to the pier. As he worked his way toward the Hudson River, there was a flurry of activity in the area as trucks and wagons made their way toward the giant ship to fill her belly with coal and her cargo holds with foodstuffs and luggage—to say nothing of cargo of every description. The *Lusitania* could ensure quick and sure delivery for people and corporations anxious to send supplies to their British friends and customers. Considered the most unsinkable ship in the world because of her speed and silhouette, it made sense to ship items of high value on the *Lusy* rather than on one of the slower cargo ships that were prone to submarine attack. Of course, the most important cargo was the mail. The suppliers and crew were so well practiced that they made it look easy, but that didn't lessen the amount of work to be done.

As Everett strolled down the street, he delighted in the smell of the ocean air in the spring. Taking another deep breath, he savored the richness of the city smells as they mingled with those of the river—even the unpleasant ones that were so repugnant to Annie—and in doing so he realized that he'd miss the chance to visit New York for meetings once his term on the board of the United States Coal Mine Owner's Association ended and he was relegated to spending the rest of his days overseeing the coal mines he owned in the West. The incongruity of this thought did not escape him, since just moments before he had been lamenting not going to Wyoming.

He was midway between major streets—the place in each block where the lighting was most subdued. Without obvious reason, the hair on the back of his neck stood up, and a shiver ran up his spine. Perhaps it was a blast of cooler air coming in from the water. "Maybe walk a little faster . . ." he whispered, not knowing why he lowered his voice. Then he heard the sound of footsteps behind him, coming too fast to casually turn and see who it was. He naturally picked up his pace, but whoever was following simply walked even faster. "Take it easy and let him pass." While that was undoubtedly the most reasonable course, it just didn't feel right, and Everett started walking so fast that it turned into a walk-run. But even that didn't do it.

The sound of the pursuer's footsteps told him the fellow was upon him, and he waited anxiously for whoever it was to pass by so he could see who it was. He wasn't to get the chance.

It's impossible to re-create the sound of the air being knocked out of your lungs. What can be said is that it leaves a person gasping helplessly for breath as a searing pain alerts the mind that the body is in trouble. In addition to the shock of losing air, Everett experienced an incredibly bright light as he was smashed from behind with such force that he barely had a moment to struggle desperately to get his hands out in front of him as he plunged toward the cobblestone street.

"What is going on!" he tried to say as his brain raced to figure out what was happening to him. But the words wouldn't come out as he still lacked sufficient air to force his vocal cords to vibrate.

"It *is* you, you blighter! I thought that was your stupid head I saw!" The words were slurred and indistinct.

As Everett crashed into the street there was a searing pain in his right wrist, and he winced at the sickening crack of a breaking bone. But that was nothing compared to the blow he then took to his ribs, which forced out any remaining air, leaving him gasping desperately to reinflate his lungs. But even in the haze of pain and surprise of what had happened, he knew that he was being mugged, which gave him just enough presence of mind to roll away from the foot that had kicked his torso. It worked for a moment, but then another blow hit him again, and he cried out in pain. As the air rushed back into his lungs, he felt that they'd burst, but at least he could breathe.

He curled into a ball, waiting for the next blow. Glancing up, he saw a dark figure standing above him, poised for another kick. But then the fellow hesitated. "I should kill you, is what I should do. Nobody would ever know." The man hesitated for a moment, and then, before he could react, Everett felt two large, powerful hands reach down and grab him by his coat collar, and the brute started to drag him into the narrow space between two brick buildings.

"Who are you?" cried Everett. "Why are you doing this to me?" He tried to hit the fellow, but the pain that shot from his arm nearly made him pass out.

"Better if you don't know."

Everett kicked at his assailant, but he must have been so disoriented that he couldn't even find that easy of a target. Instead, his shoe connected with something metal, and there was a loud clang.

"Quiet!" the man shouted.

Everett kicked again, which must have knocked the lid off, because this time there were resounding clangs of metal on cobblestone.

"I said quiet!" the assailant said as another blow crashed into Everett's ribs.

There was nothing else he could do, so he tightened up into an even tighter ball, preparing himself for the worst. "You can have my money! My wallet is in my coat pocket." He recognized the desperate sound in his voice. "There's nearly a hundred dollars in cash!" Based on the sequence of previous kicks, he knew another one was due and so he braced himself. He had to get out of this, but he couldn't figure out how. To his surprise, the next kick didn't come.

"I don't want your filthy money . . ."

Somewhere inside his aching head, his brain worked to process the voice. He'd heard it before—he knew that. But it sounded different now. "Think!" he ordered himself.

"It's you I want, you miscreant."

Miscreant? Everett thought. *Why would anyone think I'm a miscreant?* Something about the way the man said his words, even though slurred, registered again.

"*Todd*? Is that you?"

He heard a snort. "Not bad. But then I never thought you were dumb."

Everett rolled over on his side and opened his eyes. Looking up, he could see only a massive chest with a dark face above it.

"Why are you doing this to me?" Everett knew that alcohol had something to do with it. But that still didn't explain the reason for the animosity in the first place.

"Why?" The voice was a little steadier. "Why? Let's think about that. Maybe because you ruined my family? Is that a good reason? You broke my mother's heart? Is that a better reason? How about that you perverted my older sister? Do any of those sound like a good reason to you, 'Brother Stringham?'"

Everett gasped in pain as another blow hit him.

"What are you talking about?" Everett tried to say, but the words jumbled in his mouth, and he felt warm liquid drip down his cheek.

"Oh, I think you know . . ." Now Todd's voice was cold and calculating, and Everett knew that the end was near. He tried to shout for help but couldn't muster enough air. So he did the only thing left to him. He kicked his right foot as hard as he could, connecting one last time with the metallic object he'd hit before. This time he must have knocked it over, because the noise was terrific.

"Why you . . ." Todd's voice was malevolent, and Everett tried to position his arms to protect his ribs—better to lose his arm than his life.

He expected some kind of sound from Todd, since every other kick had been accompanied by a grunt, but this time there was a shrill, high-pitched noise that was totally unexpected. Then he saw a form crash into John Todd, sending him tumbling to the ground.

Todd yelled, "What the blazes?"

Everett turned as best he could to see what was going on.

"What do you think you're doing, Mr. Todd? What have you done to Mr. Stringham?" There was a desperate sound to Bill Shafer's voice.

"You stay out of this, Shafer! I'm doing it for you, you stupid dolt!"

Everett watched as Todd attempted to stand up. "You are not!" yelled Bill as he threw himself atop Todd, wrestling furiously to keep him on the ground.

"Get off me . . ." Todd tried to say, but the battle had clearly turned. Unlike Everett, Bill had not been taken by surprise, so he was fresh and alert. And he was much younger than Todd, even though he was smaller.

"What's going on there?" Everett's head reeled as yet another voice came on the scene.

"Over here! I need help!" Bill shouted. If Everett was unconscious, the dream wasn't letting him have any peace.

Everett looked up and saw the silhouette of a policeman running toward them. "What are you two up to?"

"Nothing . . ." Todd tried to say.

"He was attacking my friend. He was kicking him and—"

"Get up!" the policeman ordered. Everett had rolled yet again to see the action and watched as Bill pulled himself off Todd, using the police officer's outstretched hand for support. Todd started to get up too, but the policeman jabbed his nightstick into his chest. "Not you! You stay put!"

Then he turned to Everett. "Are you all right?"

"I think he broke my wrist and maybe a rib."

"He broke 'em," shouted Bill, and the policeman had to restrain him from going after Todd again.

"Can you sit up?" The policeman knelt down and helped Everett pull himself into a sitting position where he could lean against the wall. "We need to get you to a hospital."

"Maybe, but right now I'd just like to catch my breath." The policeman looked dubious. "I'm all right, really."

Once he was convinced, the officer turned back to Todd. "All right now, what's this all about?" Todd simply glowered at him. The policeman gave him a whack with his stick. "I asked you a question!"

"Nothing. It's personal."

"Personal? This is how you treat a person?"

"It's nothing. I'm guilty. Take me in!"

"I'll do that, all right." The policeman gave him another whack—not enough to badly hurt him, but more than enough to demonstrate that he was in control and to elicit a gasp of pain from Todd.

"Can you help your friend?" asked the policeman of Bill.

"Yes, sir. I'll be glad to. We're just a block away from our hotel. I'm sure they can help us."

"Are you all right to go that far?"

Everett nodded. By now he'd caught his breath, and he felt that perhaps his ribs weren't broken. His wrist was a different story. "I'll be all right. Bill can help me."

"Good. Then I'll take this fellow in." The policeman reached down to pull Todd up.

"Wait a minute, officer. Before you do anything, I need to talk to him."

"Talk to him?" the policeman and Bill asked in unison.

"It looks to me like he tried to kill you," said the policeman. "Why would you want to talk to him?"

Everett took a deep breath to steady himself. "Because it *is* personal—about something that I need to understand." He looked at the policeman's face. "This isn't the first time he's threatened me. Yet somehow I don't think it really has anything to do with me. I have to know why he's so angry. Please."

"We'll get his statement at the station house . . ."

"I doubt he'll tell you. Please let me talk to him. You can stand over there, and Bill can stay here by me. Bill is tied up in this too—although I don't know how."

"Well . . . this is irregular . . ."

"If he gives us trouble, you can get here in a second." Everett turned himself painfully toward Todd, and the policeman stepped away.

"I don't have anything to say to you," said Todd.

"If you don't want to go to jail and lose your job, you do."

Todd turned with a fury in his eyes. "Like I'm going to avoid that even if I do talk to you!"

"You'll avoid it if I refuse to press charges."

"And why would you do that?"

Everett coughed. He looked in the hand he used to cover his mouth to see if there was any blood, but his hand was clear.

"Because I want to know what you meant when you talked about your mother and sister. I want to know it badly enough to let you off the hook if you promise not to hurt me again."

Todd hesitated. "Why should I trust you?"

"Because he's an honest man!" said Bill. "And too kind at that. He's not rubbish like you."

"This won't stop until we get him to talk. If you provoke him, that won't happen. Let me handle this. Please."

Bill drew in his breath but then relented. "All right. But if he tries to hurt you—"

"—you'll protect me. Now, Mr. Todd. What is this all about?"

"About? It's about . . ." To their surprise, John Todd actually choked up. Not from fear but with emotion in his voice.

"Is it about your sister? What about your sister?"

Todd jerked his head around, and fire flashed in his eyes. "How do you know about my sister?"

"Because you told me about her—when you were beating the sense out of me."

"My sister . . ." Todd pursed his lips.

"Talk to him, Mr. Todd. You answer Mr. Stringham's questions or else!"

"Fine!" Todd exploded. "You want to know about my sister? I'll tell you. The Mormon missionaries came to Liverpool thirty years ago. I was just ten years old, she was twenty. And they converted her to their sect. The next thing we knew, they took her off to Utah to be married as the third wife of the missionary who 'converted' her!" He choked on his rage. "And it broke my mother's heart. My father disowned her. I was told to never talk about her again—and after that our lives were never the same!" Now there was sincere sorrow manifest in his voice. "You people ruined our family, and I never saw her again." To their astonishment, Todd started sobbing. "They took her away . . ."

"Oh, dear heavens," said Everett as Bill exclaimed, "They did that? They took people away?" The shock was very evident in his voice.

"Yes, they did that, you stupid fool. And they'll do it to you, too. Except that you'll get to be the man with all those wives." He looked up, choking back the emotion. "And how many wives do you have, Mr. Stringham? How many women did you take home with you from England!?"

The color drained from Everett's face.

"They don't still do polygamy, do they?" Bill asked desperately.

Everett shook his head. "No. They haven't practiced it for twenty years."

"I've heard that rubbish before. But what does it do for my sister? What became of her when they did away with polygamy—if they really did?"

Everett turned toward John Todd. "I am sorry for the pain you've suffered. I understand your anger now. I wish I could do something." The distress in Everett's voice was so sincere that it knocked even John Todd off balance.

"Well, sorry doesn't pay the bill, does it?"

Everett shook his head. "I'm sure there is nothing, except God's love, that can help you and your family. I know I don't have the words."

"So, is he right? Did missionaries do that—come to England to find wives?"

"To find beautiful young girls," said Todd contemptuously.

"Missionaries did come to England, and polygamy was part of the doctrine of the Church for some fifty years. But no one was authorized to come looking for a wife."

"But that's what that blighter did . . ."

Everett took another deep breath. "Can I tell you a few things, Mr. Todd? Maybe they'll give you comfort."

"You can tell me what's become of my sister! You can tell me how her life is ruined." He hesitated. "Or maybe don't tell me. Maybe it's better if I don't know."

"What did become of his sister?" Now it was Bill who had an accusing tone.

Everett raised his left hand to try to calm them down. Todd glowered, but Bill, who had moved slightly closer to Todd and away from Everett, replied quickly, "I want to know. I have to know."

"Do you want to know, Mr. Todd?"

"What's going on over there?" The policeman's voice betrayed his impatience.

"Just another minute," replied Everett. "We may not need to press charges. Can you give me just another minute?"

"Not press charges!"

"I don't know yet. But we're making progress." Everett stalled for time. Then quietly, "Will you listen to me, in exchange for your freedom? I'm just trying to help you."

"I still don't believe you."

"Why would I lie? What do I have to gain? I can have you arrested right now if I want.

Todd didn't say anything.

"Did you ever try to reach out to your sister? To find out how she's doing?"

"That's none of your business."

"Before you beat a man to death, it seems like you would at least make the attempt to find her. Did she ever communicate with you?"

Todd dropped his voice. "She wrote letters. My mother would read them and then burn them. If my father ever saw them . . . It doesn't change anything . . ."

"You're right. The fact is that your sister joined an obscure church, left England, and you've never seen her since . . . that can never change. I understand why that hurts, and so you wanted to hurt me. I can't do anything about *that*. And your beating me does nothing to help your sister, if she needs help. If you really love her, then you ought to let me help you, rather than trying to hurt me."

"Help me? How can you help me?"

Everett took a long breath. All this talking was difficult, and his ribs felt like a red-hot firebrand in his side. But he had to force himself to keep talking. "I live in Wyoming, just two hours from Salt Lake City by train. If you give me her name, and maybe the last address you had for her, I'm sure I can find her. I'm a man of means, and I can help her if she needs it.

"The main point is that I could tell her you are alive and that you love her. I think that would do more for her than anything money could do. I could even arrange to host you if you came to see her." Everett paused to see how his offer would be received.

"I couldn't come out there. She'd hate me for ignoring her all these years."

"Was that the kind of person she was before she left?"

Todd glanced over at him. "She was wonderful. That's why it hurt us all so much."

"People who are wonderful don't stop being wonderful. I imagine that her trials and sorrows have made her even kinder than she was. I feel confident that she'd love to see you."

"I . . . I don't know how I feel about that."

"What's it to be?" the policeman called over to them. "I need to take this fellow in."

Everett knew his time was short. It was now or never. "Tell me what it's to be, John. If you promise to leave me and Bill alone, I won't press charges."

"And why wouldn't you? I nearly killed you." Now there was fear in John Todd's voice.

Everett hesitated. "Because I understand your anger. I can put myself in your place and know why you were hurt. I can imagine that I would want to strike back myself. And yet it all could have been different. You travel to the United States regularly. You could have sent her a telegram. You could have sent her money to come see you in New York, if you didn't want to go to Salt Lake City. You could tell her about your life and learn about hers."

"But I didn't, did I?"

"But you still can. That's the point."

Todd looked uncertain, as if he wanted to cooperate, but still he hesitated.

"Come on," the policeman said, striding over to them. "I'm taking this guy in. And you need to get to a doctor. There's been enough talking."

"No!" said Everett. He'd hoped to extract a promise from Todd but hadn't received it. So now he needed to act on faith. His heart told him that he needed to accept the risk. "It will do you no good to take him in because I won't press charges. And you weren't here to see the fight, so a judge would have to dismiss any charges you bring."

"You are a fool!" said the policeman. "The man nearly killed you."

"And I will not press charges. It's that simple."

"What about this fellow? He saw what happened!"

Everett turned to Bill. "He did. And he has been a victim of Mr. Todd's anger as well. Bill, it's up to you. You can decide to press charges if you like, but I hope you won't. I think Mr. Todd deserves another chance."

The color now drained from Bill's face. He turned to Todd, who simply stared blankly.

"They don't need to press charges. I did it," Todd said.

"Don't!" said Bill. "Mr. Stringham's right." He glanced back at Everett. Bill looked up at the policeman, and with a maturity beyond his years, he said, "I think this man has already paid a terrible price for what he did tonight. It's just that he paid it in advance. He's been suffering from it for thirty years. Going to jail won't make it right." He looked over to Everett, who nodded. "I think only God can make it right." Then Bill turned to John Todd. "Let us make it right, Mr. Todd. Let Mr. Stringham help you and your sister."

Everett drew a deep breath. The worst was over now. There was hope for John Todd. More importantly, Bill Shafer had stood up like a man and made the right choice.

"Fine!" said the policeman. "I believe you're all a bunch of fools." He hesitated. "Are you sure you don't want me to take him in?"

Everett shook his head. "We'll be all right." With that, the policeman turned and made his way back to the street.

Everett's head was pounding, and now he noticed the searing pain in his wrist. His ribs hurt. But somehow his heart felt light. That's when he heard the muffled sobs next to him. In spite of his own pain, he motioned for Bill to help John Todd.

Chapter 13
The German Warning

May 1, 1915—New York City

NOTICE!

Travelers intending to embark on the Atlantic voyage are reminded that a state of war exists between Germany and her allies and Great Britain and her allies; that the zone of war includes the waters adjacent to the British Isles; that, in accordance with formal notice given by the Imperial German Government, vessels flying the flag of Great Britain, or any of her allies, are liable to destruction in those waters and that travelers sailing in the war zone on the ships of Great Britain or her allies do so at their own risk.

IMPERIAL GERMAN EMBASSY
Washington, DC

The *Lusitania* was British, even though earlier that year it had, for a voyage or two, flown under an American flag by order of the ship's captain—albeit without the consent of the United States government. That action caused a howl of protest from the Wilson administration in Washington, DC, since the Germans could easily consider the use of an American flag on a British-owned ship a formal alliance, swiftly negating American neutrality. When the *Lusitania* was built in 1906, it received a generous subsidy from the British Admiralty so that it could be quickly converted into wartime service, if required.

This included special gun mounts to aid in surface action. While still in passenger service, the ship had not taken on guns, although the Germans expressed their belief that it had. As a result of America's protest, the American flag was taken down, and the Cunard Line had been forced to develop other strategies to protect the ship. For example, they'd painted the smokestacks black, instead of displaying the proud colors of Cunard Line; they'd painted over her name; and, for most of each voyage, they sailed with no flag. Anything to make it more difficult for the Germans to identify her.

* * *

Everett Stringham nursed his right arm as he stepped painfully out of the cab at Pier 54. "What's all the commotion?" he asked this of a newspaper boy who came running up to him.

"Commotion? Why, mister, the Germans have said they are going to sink the *Lusitania*! It's right here in the *New York Times*! Buy a copy and read it for yourself."

"Go away!" said Bill Shafer, but Everett reached into his pocket to grab a coin for the boy. The dime he handed him was more than the nickel the paper cost, and when the boy realized that he was to keep the change, he quickly said, "Thanks, mister!" and was on his way, shouting, "Extra, extra! Read all about it! Germans issue warning! It's printed on the same page as the *Lusitania*'s sailing schedule!"

"What a pest," said Bill.

"Controversy sells newspapers." Everett tried to open the paper to the spot indicated but he hadn't figured out how to use his left arm by this point so his right wrist could heal. He was deadly tired, having spent most of the night up with the doctor, and tried to stifle a yawn as his thoughts wandered to the events of the previous night. After gaining control of his temper, John Todd had helped Bill get Everett back to the hotel, apologizing yet again while promising to turn himself in the next morning. When he finally figured out that Everett was truly not going to press charges and really was willing to forgive him, he lapsed into a silence that was almost impenetrable—a kind of agony playing across his face as he struggled to understand what was happening to him.

Bill had wondered too, expressing his indignation that Todd should get off scot-free.

"He's felt hurt all these years for what his sister did to him, and then it turned to guilt when he did nothing to reach out to her," Everett explained. "That's a lot to try a man's soul. Last night he just lost control, and now he feels guilty for that."

"So Mr. Todd is feeling guilty for what he did to you?"

"I think Mr. Todd is feeling tormented by a lot of things."

Bill shook his head and shrugged his shoulders. "I still think he should have gone to jail. He beat you, after all . . ."

"If you hadn't come along, he probably would have killed me." Everett paused. "I hope I told you thank you for defending me."

"You did."

"So I understand why it's confusing. The simple answer is that I think he'll be all right. Now that he's gotten all of that out in the open, I think he will make peace with it. Right now he just needs some time with his own thoughts."

After helping Everett to the hotel, where a doctor was summoned, Todd had eventually excused himself, disappearing into the early morning. Everett managed to get a couple of fitful hours of sleep, waking each time he rolled onto his right arm. But he no longer felt threatened and even felt satisfaction that in a crisis as dire as this, he had managed to keep his head.

Returning to the present, Everett asked, "Bill, can you help me with this newspaper?"

"I don't think you should read it. The Germans are just bluffing, you know."

A fellow standing in the line nearby nodded his agreement. "It's all a big farce to scare us off. Everyone knows the British Admiralty will protect us."

Another person added his piece. "It's criminal, really, that the newspapers would even publish such a thing. It doesn't matter how much the Germans paid for the advertisement. It's still uncivilized."

"So you all think that the Germans are doing this only for propaganda's sake?" asked Everett.

"I guess that answers the question, doesn't it?" said the first fellow, pointing to a spot behind them. Everett and the others turned to see an elegantly dressed gentleman step out of a Fiat automobile, which, at $30,000, was one of the most expensive automobiles in the world.

"If Alfred Vanderbilt is coming on board, I guess he knows what's up with the Germans."

Everett raised an eyebrow. "So that's the infamous Alfred Vanderbilt—industrialist, philanthropist, and philanderer?"

The others laughed. "It's true that he's a well-known playboy and one of the richest men in the world. It's said that he's worth $100 million. You can count on the fact that he wouldn't sail on the *Lusy* if he thought there was any chance of a German attack."

Everett sighed. "Well, I really have no choice. I can't wait any longer, so I guess I have to sail whether the Germans issue a warning or not."

"Good show!" said one of the men.

"We'll show them we won't be intimidated," added another.

"It's like we're part of the war effort—keeping the shipping lanes open," added a third.

Everett marveled how people facing deadly peril could talk themselves into believing that it was a patriotic duty to sail on a passenger ship going into harm's way, even when they were businessmen, not soldiers.

"Listen, Mr. Stringham," said Bill quietly. "I need to go on board. I'm already late. And if Mr. Todd has been here, I may not be welcome."

"If Mr. Todd has been here and given you any trouble, I'll pay your fare and hire you as my personal valet. They can't prevent that." Everett looked around. "Besides, I think you need to have a little more faith. Perhaps Mr. Todd has had a change of heart."

"I'm not sure. But I'd better go. I hope I don't have to take you up on your offer. Not that I wouldn't be honored to serve as your valet; it's just that you've already spent way too much money on me, and I hope you don't have to spend any more."

Bill started off, and Everett returned to his newspaper. He was waiting in a short line for embarkation orders, which is why he was startled when Bill came bounding back just a few moments later.

"I have my answer," he said breathlessly. "I'm still on the roster."

As Everett started to say, "That was fast," John Todd came into view. The man looked as if he'd aged ten years since the last time they'd seen him.

"Mr. Todd . . ." said Everett.

John Todd approached cautiously and kept his distance when Bill positioned himself between Todd and Everett. Then he politely inquired if Everett would step out of the line.

"Listen, Mr. Stringham. I don't remember everything that happened last night. I had been drinking way too much. But I do remember hurting you, and I do remember what you said about my sister. I most certainly remember that you refused to press charges, even though I did not promise not to hurt you again."

"Somehow I felt I'd be all right."

"Well," said Todd, looking around nervously, "that's the whole point. I'm willing to make that promise now." He swallowed hard. "And I'm willing to resign my position with Cunard, if you like. I clearly have no right to serve on a ship after treating a passenger the way I treated you."

"You know I wouldn't ask that of you. If you promise me, then I accept your promise at face value."

Todd looked around again nervously. "If that's the way you feel, it will actually be good for Cunard. With all these threats from the Germans and so many of the young men serving in the British navy, we're badly understaffed." He hesitated. "And I can make certain Bill Shafer is your steward, if you like."

Everett opened and closed his mouth as recognition dawned. This was Todd's peace offering. He had taken Bill away on the first crossing to isolate him from the threat of getting involved with Mormons. Allowing him to serve Everett on this crossing was Todd's way of acknowledging their conversation and a change of heart. "Of course. I'd like that. I assume you'll be my head steward."

"I . . ." Todd shook his head. "I just don't understand how you can do this? I beat you and kicked you . . . to within an inch of your life! How can you be like this?"

Everett reached out his left arm and rested his hand on Todd's shoulder. "There is much about the Mormons you don't understand, and while you don't have to learn about our doctrine or accept our missionaries, you do need to know that we try to follow in Christ's footsteps. I believe that He would forgive you for what happened last night because He understands what drove you to it. And if He would forgive you, then I will forgive you."

"You're certainly right that I don't understand. But I do know now that you are an honest man, so I will accept what you tell me."

"Then the two of you better be off. I'm sure you've got lots of work to do. I'll be fine out here." He motioned for Bill to go ahead, which he did, although he hesitated for a moment at the thought of leaving Everett alone with Todd.

"I'm glad we worked this out," said Everett.

Todd turned to leave. Then he turned back. "About my sister . . ."

"I'll be glad to look her up. Just give me whatever information you have, and I promise to let you know what I find."

"Thank you." Before he could show any more emotion, Todd turned and quickly strode toward the ship.

Everett returned to his place in the line. A moment later, as a Cunard officer happened by, he noticed his bandaged arm. "You are hurt, Mr. Stringham! May I offer you special assistance?"

Everett was always amazed at how these people could remember names so well.

"Actually, I'd like that. I am feeling a little drained."

The officer extended his right arm so Everett could lean on it with his left arm. As they passed up the line, Everett overheard a local police officer say to one of the *Lusitania*'s young bellboys, "You're not going to get back this time, sonny. They're going to get you this time." The boy tried to stammer a reply, but the man quickly disappeared into the crowd when he saw the ship officer.

"Do you put much stock in this warning?" asked Everett.

"*Poppycock* is the word I think I heard the captain use," replied the officer. He helped Everett lift himself up onto the gangplank. "It's virtually impossible for a submarine to catch the *Lusy*. Besides, we'll be sailing under Admiralty orders, which means we're under their protection as well. The biggest problem you'll face on this trip is learning to do things with your left hand." The officer appeared very seasoned, and he said all this with an almost preternatural calm that soothed Everett's nerves.

"I hope so," he said. Yet with everything that had happened, he couldn't help but feel anxious.

"There we go, Mr. Stringham." The officer helped Everett step onto the deck. He then raised his hand to catch the eye of one of the stewards. "Would you please help Mr. Stringham to his cabin? Make sure he's settled comfortably and get him some food and refreshment."

"Thank you. This really is a help."

"We do our best, sir. Perhaps I'll see you again on the voyage."

As Everett and the younger man made their way toward the first-class elevator, Everett felt himself go light-headed. At the steward's entreaty, he allowed himself to be seated in a deck chair while the steward went in search of a wheelchair.

As he settled in, he let himself relax. Knowing that he would not be at odds with John Todd any longer took a great load off his mind. In time, he started enjoying himself as he watched the embarking passengers make their way past him, noting to himself when someone of particular prominence happened by. Charles Frohman, the greatest producer of musical theater on either side of the Atlantic, walked by Everett. He recalled that in the director's notes for the Frohman play he had attended with Annie in London, it had been mentioned that Frohman traveled to Europe every spring to scout out British plays that might do well on Broadway, as well as to take his own ideas to London's West End theater district.

Everett recognized the famous Quaker explorer Commander David Stackhouse, who had been in the newspapers recently for his efforts to lead the British Antarctic and Oceanographical Expedition to survey the coastline of Antarctica. He continued to watch as elegantly dressed women and finely attired gentlemen whom he did not recognize strolled past on their way to their first-class cabins.

Then he saw someone he knew. "David! David Thomas!" The former liberal member of Parliament turned at the sound of his name.

"Everett Stringham! I didn't know you'd be on this crossing." He came striding across the deck to greet Everett. "But you've injured your wrist."

"Nothing serious. Painful, but it will heal."

A beautiful young woman came up by Thomas. "May I present my daughter."

Everett stood up, unsteadily. "A pleasure. I have a daughter who must be near your age, and seeing you reminds me of her."

The young woman smiled but demurred to answer.

"So how's the American coal business?" asked Thomas. He was

a Welsh coal magnate with a great fortune that was undoubtedly growing greater with all the demands of the war.

"We're doing well. Lots of ships at sea, and lots of manufacturing that needs energy."

"Same for us. We can't get it out of the ground fast enough. We have the additional problem of many of our young men being drafted, which leaves us understaffed, and I think it's a problem that's only going to worsen." Thomas beckoned to his manservant who had been standing nearby. "We better get going. Perhaps we can have dinner, Stringham. I'd love to catch up on your activities here. In fact, I'd be pleased to make any introductions you might require."

"Thank you. I appreciate that." Everett started to stand up in respect for Thomas's daughter, but she begged him to sit back down. As he settled in, his wrist throbbed.

"Sorry to take so long, Mr. Stringham." The steward came forward confidently pushing a wicker wheelchair. "I had to go down a couple of decks."

"I've enjoyed sitting here watching the passengers, so no harm done. But now I'm ready to lie down." The steward helped him get settled in the wheelchair and then started pushing him toward the elevator. "There's quite a buzz on the ship, what with this German warning."

"I haven't seen it myself," replied the steward. "I've been up most of the night getting ready. But it is causing some anxiety." He paused as he turned the wheelchair around to back it through one of the portals. "But I wouldn't put too much stock in it, if I were you. I think it's more of a warning to the American government to stay out of it. But then, what do I know? It's up to the Admiralty to protect us."

Everett didn't say anything, but he questioned the logic of those who talked of Admiralty protection. Why should they trust the same government that started the mess to protect them now that the war effort was so desperate?

"Here we are, sir. Your cabin is ready and waiting." Rather than make the poor fellow back the chair through the door, Everett stood up and stepped into the room. It was a nicely appointed cabin, rather than the suite he had purchased when traveling with Annie. This would actually be more comfortable for a single person traveling alone.

"I'm afraid we're a little understaffed. The war keeps taking the young men away from us, and, I'm embarrassed to say, not a few of our crew abandon service when they get in America. My understanding is that Mr. Todd is out recruiting even this very moment." He hastened to add, "Of course, that would be for steerage and the lower grades—the most experienced stewards will be used to service those of you in first class."

Everett smiled. "Of course. Thank you." He handed the steward a quarter tip.

"No need, sir. We're tipped at the end."

"Ah, yes, but you may not be my steward. And I desperately needed your help. I hope you'll accept it as my thanks."

"Thank you, then, sir. Have a good voyage."

Chapter 14
Of Submarines and Poison Gas

May 2, 1915 —Orkney Islands, North of Scotland

"At last, we've reached the northernmost point of our voyage after 1,200 kilometers through the cursed North Sea. Now we can turn south and into the hunting grounds."

U-20 submarine captain Walther Schweiger glanced at his pilot, Lanz, who responded, "If the English Channel weren't so narrow and easily defended, we could cut the distance by two-thirds."

Schweiger sneered. "But while that would save us some trouble, my dear Lanz, it would also make life a lot easier for the Royal Navy, since they could concentrate their forces there. As it is, we have them stretched out from Greece to Scotland. So our long detour serves a purpose, after all."

"Why would anyone want to live in this godforsaken place? Scrub brush and sand dunes. Nothing to rival the beauty of Germany."

"True, but an almost perfect anchorage for the Royal Navy's heavy ships. A nice, sandy bottom and a group of islands to protect the harbor. It's just as perfect now for the British North Sea fleet as it was for the Vikings a thousand years ago. I'll be glad when we're past it."

A short silence ensued, broken once again by the pilot. "Wouldn't it be marvelous to get inside the base at Scapa Flow and shoot all our torpedoes at those battleships and destroyers? We could blast our way right into history." Lanz was a well-known expert on all ships British with an almost uncanny ability to quickly identify the type and class of a ship by its silhouette, including smokestack, superstructure, and bow. He could often name the specific ship, if it was at all prominent, and cite its normal and top speeds. In other words, he was absolutely invaluable.

Schweiger shook his head. "We'd make it into history, all right. Just like *U-14* last year. Rammed by a trawler as it tried to make its way into the anchorage." He turned and looked at Lanz. "A rather ignominious way to die, don't you think? They didn't get the chance to fire a single torpedo, so the entire crew drowned for nothing." Before the man could interrupt, Schweiger added, "I prefer fat merchant ships. That's what's going to bring down the Allies. Cut Britain off from her suppliers around the world, and all that's left is a pathetic little island with no more ability to make war than Lichtenstein." He motioned for Lanz to step closer. "We're also interested in troop transports. I was briefed just as we were leaving Wilhelmshaven that with all the British activity in the Dardanelles in the Mediterranean, we can expect to see many troop transports. That's to be our very highest priority." He straightened up so the lookouts above him wouldn't become curious. "So be patient, my friend. We don't need to sink battleships. We need to sink the merchant marine. All it takes is patience."

A distinct sound of barking came up through the hatch from inside the boat. "Our little family is making a ruckus. I should go look after them," said Schweiger. On an earlier voyage he had adopted a dachshund that his men had rescued after *U-20* had sunk a Portuguese sailing ship. She had then given birth to a litter of puppies that now had free run of the ship. The men loved the dogs, and Schweiger appreciated the fact that it helped provide a sense of home and normalcy while out on a cruise.

* * *

May 3, 1915—Lusitania

"HOW CAN THE GERMAN HIGH Command possibly condone this sort of thing? It's yet another outrage," said a London man named Moulton, with whom Everett breakfasted.

Everett glanced up from the orange marmalade he'd been spreading on a piece of toast.

A fellow American at the table named Andrew Haws asked, "What new outrage is that?"

"Chlorine gas used on our troops at Ypres. Can you imagine

stooping so low as to poison people? They suffocate! It's a horrible way to die and a direct violation of the Hague Treaty. Apparently there is no depth to which German treachery will not descend."

"I've read about it," said Everett. "It is, indeed, a revolting development."

"I think it's another example of their desperation," said Haws, a haberdasher from New York City who was on his way to Europe to see what fine men's clothing he could buy for his men's clothing store. Even though France, Russia, and England were locked in a life-and-death duel with Germany, they still needed international trade to keep their citizens alive and to keep enough cash flowing to finance the war. And New Yorkers still had money to spend on clothing.

"You think the Germans are desperate?" asked Everett skeptically. "From all the accounts I've read, it certainly seems they're holding their own."

"Why else would they initiate all this talk about unrestricted warfare on the seas and gas on the battlefield? If a nation can't win fairly, then they should withdraw from the field of battle."

Moulton nodded his assent, but Everett shook his head in disbelief. "I think you're both a bit naive. Our American Civil War showed that there is no honor left in war. Looting and pillaging on a grand scale, with cities like Atlanta burned to the ground and her citizens left to starve. There is no glory nor chivalry in modern war." When neither man responded, he added, "Still, this use of gas is taking war to a new low. As a mine owner, I'm aware of how insidious gas is and the terrible complications it causes even for those who survive."

"It's those cursed trenches!" said Moulton vehemently. "Two great armies churning each other up in a meat grinder as tens of thousands die. More than 60,000 killed in one day! The Kaiser should be ashamed for unleashing such an injustice on the world."

Everett decided he didn't like this Englishman who saw the issues as simple black-and-white. "Forgive me, but unless I'm mistaken, it takes an opponent to make a war. As an American I cannot understand why there aren't any adults to make the squabbling kings, kaisers, and czars pick up their toys and play nicely with one another. It's clear now that Germany isn't going to conquer France in six weeks as planned, just as it is equally clear that the Allies aren't going to abandon the battlefield. So why not negotiate a return to things as they were? This war should have never started in the first place."

Moulton grumbled. "Easy for an American to say, but do you honestly believe that a person should stand by and watch a bully beat up a friend? We went to war over Belgium neutrality. And France was in desperate straits."

"Again, with due respect, it seems to many in America that there are a lot of bullies in Europe—all three of the belligerents have far-flung empires that were wrested from the native peoples with overwhelming force. Now that you're up against each other, it's a fair fight—a foolish fight—but a fair one."

Moulton glowered, and Haws dropped his gaze. Everett knew immediately that he'd come on too strong. After all, it was nearly impossible for Moulton or any other Englishman to express any sentiment but loyalty to England's cause.

"I am sorry, Mr. Moulton. Having chosen to remain neutral, we Americans really should keep our noses out of your business. This is a great ordeal for your country and I am sensitive to the sacrifices. And to the degree that there is a 'right' side in this war, you are on it."

Moulton glanced up, his breathing slowing. "No need to apologize. I have considered everything you've said myself. But I'm afraid we're into it, and there's no way out but to push on. If we fail to check Germany this time, she'll just be back in the future." He fumbled with his food for a moment. "I just wish that America would commit herself. Perhaps just the threat of American involvement would be enough to cow the Germans into negotiations. As it is, they feel they have the stronger hand." He shuffled again. "And perhaps they do. If so, I hope that one day your neutrality will yield to our cause."

"It's not as simple as that," said Haws. "Even though our government claims to be neutral, my German customers don't think America is neutral at all. They are outraged that we continue to trade with the Allied countries while honoring the British blockade of Germany. They think it patently unfair."

"That's part of the problem," added Everett. "There is no consensus in the United States. For example, the Irish-Americans are all on the side of Germany."

"Because they are in harmony with anyone who is against England?" Moulton responded.

"Exactly. And we also have a very large population with German ancestry. So our leaders would be hard-pressed to make a case for going to war on behalf of the Allies. To most Americans this is just another round in an interminable contest of European wars that go back more than a thousand years."

"But this war is different," said Moulton. "We didn't go seeking this war. The Kaiser did! King Edward even made a personal appeal to Wilhelm—they're cousins, you know—but to no avail. Now it is a matter of honor to see it out."

Everett sighed. "And so it goes. At any rate, I'm very sorry to hear that the Germans have started using chlorine gas. The real tragedy is that it's remarkably ineffective, and yet a man can still die from it if he doesn't know how to respond. It must be terrifying to the troops."

"What do you mean, ineffective?" asked Haws.

"The gas sinks. So once the canisters are fired, the greenish cloud of chlorine flows across the surface of the ground and then down into the trenches. If a man happens to be lying there asleep, he is likely to die from it. But if he stands up, his risk goes down dramatically. From what I've read, the men who are stationed in the parapets at the top of the trenches suffer almost no ill effects. So the Germans have unleashed a weapon that brings shame on them, and that may lead to even more horrible weaponized gases, and all for very little military advantage. They really do run the risk of being labeled barbarians."

Moulton motioned to their waiter. "Yes, sir?"

"Could I have another cup of that delicious coffee?"

"Certainly, sir. More for you gentlemen?"

Haws nodded, but Everett demurred.

"I hope you'll forgive me for changing the subject," said Moulton, "but the truth is that too much talk about the war gives me stomach trouble."

"Particularly when you encounter an insensitive codger like me," said Everett.

Moulton smiled. "Yes, well, it's very shallow of me, but one of the reasons I love traveling to America is for the abundance of food and drink you have there." He took a long, savory sip of the coffee, which he had carefully creamed and sugared. He held up the cup. "Like this coffee. We can't get this in England—it's not worth taking up room on the transport ships. But since the *Lusitania* has to stock up in New York anyway, her passengers are indulged." He smiled.

"Crossing an ocean in wartime seems an awfully dangerous way to get a cup of coffee, don't you think?" asked Everett.

Moulton smiled again. "I suppose. But I still think the *Lusitania* is invulnerable. Even if they should get off the most lucky torpedo shot in the world and hit us, which I think is impossible—but even if they did that, the ship is still unsinkable. There would be plenty of time to get help." He took a last drink out of the cup. "So it's worth the inconvenience, should it happen."

Everett smiled. He did love the British dry sense of humor.

* * *

"GOOD EVENING, SIR." SINCE RETURNING to duty, Bill had gone back to his formal way of addressing Everett.

"Good evening, Bill."

"I won't be but a minute." He hesitated. "But I can leave off now if you prefer."

"No, I like it when you do turndown service. Please go ahead."

Bill returned to his work, and Everett reached behind his neck to loosen the black bow tie that was part of his tuxedo. It was expected that everyone in first class would dress formally for dinner. Although a bit inconvenient, Everett enjoyed looking smart and stylish, and he loved the fact that everyone at dinner took the trouble to appear at their best.

Loosening his cummerbund, he let out a sigh. Dinner had been a lavish affair, with caviar and crackers, an outstanding assortment of cheeses and fruit, and a main course of chateaubriand steak (which he dearly loved) served with small potatoes. Although he had all the beef he could desire in Wyoming, it was never prepared with such distinction. "I guess I am a bit of a snob like Moulton," he said to himself.

"What was that, sir?" Everett glanced over to Bill.

"Nothing. I was just talking to myself. A habit of old people, I suppose. I was just reflecting on what a wonderful meal I was served tonight."

"I'm glad to hear it. Cunard was somewhat behind, on that front, until the *Lusitania* came into service. We were known for our speed more than our amenities. That's why we were losing passengers to Hamburg-Amerika."

"Well, your chef more than made up for it tonight, I can assure you."

Bill smiled, which pleased Everett. "By the way, does the crew eat the same food that we passengers eat?"

"What?" Bill's eyes widened in astonishment. "Of course not! We get very plain fare. Although to be fair, I have to say that we get plenty of food. That's one of the advantages of serving on the *Lusy*. We eat better than any of our countrymen at home, except of course for the aristocracy."

"Too bad. You'd have enjoyed it tonight."

Bill nodded but didn't reply.

"There you are!" Bill slapped the pillow on Everett's bed. "All set for a restful night's sleep."

"Thank you." Everett pondered what he might say. He really didn't want Bill to leave yet. "By the way, does it seem to you that we're going more slowly than usual?"

Bill nodded. "I'm not supposed to say anything, since it might worry the passengers. But Avery tells me they're running on a limited number of boilers again and that his supervisors are on them to conserve coal."

"I can see why that would worry people. We did pay full price, after all, and we expect a timely crossing."

"I'm sure that's not . . ." Bill started to say, flustered.

"Don't worry. I'm not one of them. From my point of view, it gives me more time to enjoy the crossing." He said this as pleasantly as possible to calm Bill down. But even he couldn't keep some anxiety out of his voice when he added, "But I do hope they'll bring us up to full steam once we enter the war zone."

"Yes, sir. I'm sure they will." Bill made his way to the door. "Well, then . . ."

"Yes. Good night."

Once the door was closed and Everett was alone, he sat down on the side of the bed and leaned down to loosen his shoes, a difficult proposition with his injured wrist. His feet hurt, even though he'd done very little walking, since his formal shoes were very stiff and tight. As he rubbed his right foot with his good left hand, he couldn't help but sigh. He suddenly felt quite lonely and far from home.

* * *

BILL WINCED AS HE TURNED the corner to the row of boilers where Avery was slaving away. The roar of the furnaces was like an unholy wailing right out of the depths of the underworld. Being below the waterline, this area had no natural lighting, and the light of the lamps that did shine was nearly extinguished by the coal dust in the air. Yet, for all the gloom, it was a fascinating place, where gigantic machines brought life and motion to the 44,000-ton ship as it sliced its way through the frigid waters of the North Atlantic. But without the hard labor of these men who worked in these hellish conditions, not a single light would shine, no fans would turn to bring ventilation to the compartments, and no steam would flow into the Parsons turbines that even now were spinning quietly behind them.

"You there! What are you doing here?"

Bill nearly jumped out of his skin as his reverie was interrupted. "I'm here to see Mr. Shafer. Permission granted by Mr. Todd," Bill said with as much confidence as he could muster.

"Then get on with it and stop standing here in the aisle like an idiot. There are *men* working *here*." The sneer in his voice was obvious as he stretched out the word *heeere,* drawing the distinction that those who served as stewards weren't real men and didn't do real work. It was an insult that Bill chose not to dignify with a response.

"Yes, sir!" he said crisply. He quickly moved two more rows over and made a right. There at the end was Avery in the act of rearranging a new load of coal that had been dumped at his feet on the filthy floor. Bill made his way through the piles of coal, doing his best not to choke to death on the acrid dust filling the air. He smiled as Avery looked up.

"Hey, little brother! What brings you down here?" Avery motioned to a backup shoveler to stand in for a moment. Such men were needed in case one of the regulars had to go to the bathroom—a practice which was frowned on but was sometimes unavoidable.

"You're going to kill yourself down here . . ."

Avery motioned for them to move over to a corner past the boilers, where it was a bit quieter. "Not today, I'm not. It's actually a piece of cake on this voyage. The captain hasn't had us at anything like full steam the whole trip. I'm going to have to start lifting weights if I hope to get my muscles back."

Bill laughed. Avery had the biggest chest of any man in their part of Liverpool. He was as strong as an ox and built very much like one.

"Now what is it that's important enough to risk a glare from my supervisor?"

"Ship's business, actually. There's a problem with the heating system in one of the staterooms, and the passenger is throwing a fit. Engineering says they are so shorthanded they can't get to it for at least an hour. Mr. Todd is beside himself, so I suggested that you could fix it. You're an engineer, at heart. So he got permission to send me down here. I thought your shift was about to end."

"It is. But I'm in no condition to go into a stateroom. Just look at me." He was a sight, indeed. The coal dust had melded with his sweaty torso so that it looked like he had dipped himself in a barrel of crude oil.

"You don't need to worry about that. There's a service corridor where the plumbing is exposed. Mr. Todd has all the tools."

"But I'll get in trouble with engineering for stepping onto their turf . . ."

"Not with John Todd covering you. It may actually work to your advantage." Bill dropped his gaze for just a moment. "Maybe mine, too. I have some fences to mend with Mr. Todd."

Avery tipped his head. "So this would be a feather in your cap?"

Bill nodded, not knowing how Avery would react. Sometimes he was more than willing to help; other times he'd take the labor line that he was to stick strictly to what his craft did and not meddle in anyone else's affairs.

"Well, it's against my better judgment, but if it will help my little brother, then I'll do it."

For the second time, Bill was startled out of his wits when the shift horn blasted through the clamor. Avery laughed. "Calm down, it's just a horn. Let's go."

As they walked past Avery's supervisor, they heard him mutter, "Nice way to spend a shift, Shafer. If you could only shovel coal as well as you can shovel words . . ."

"I'm sorry . . ." Bill started to explain, but Avery shushed him.

"They got their fair work out of me. Don't ever kowtow to a boss—not when you're doing your job." Avery tipped his head at the fellow and gave him an exaggerated smile. His supervisor simply shook his head in disgust but didn't make anything more of it.

As they made their way to the service elevator, Avery stopped to wash his hands and put a shirt on. "They tell me there's this bright light up there that's harmful to vampires and shovelers. If I get exposed to it, pull me back before I shrivel up and die."

"We call it the sun," replied Bill. "I'll shield you from it so it doesn't suck your soul out. But not to worry—I think I can take you through enough back corridors that you won't need to worry about either the sun or that other enemy to men like you—fresh air."

"You'd do that for me?" Avery gave him a light punch on the shoulder. "You're an all-right fellow."

As they made their way up a couple of levels, Avery was confident that his younger brother hadn't shown him anything new. But then, with a twist here and a diversion there, he found himself moving down unfamiliar corridors. "Are you sure you know where you're taking me?"

Bill nodded. "We could use the elevators, but they're not always safe. I'd hate to get stuck in one. This is a less-traveled route that can take you to all the key points on the ship. Occasionally we'll pass near the passenger compartments, so try not to dust anything as you pass by."

Avery laughed. "Easier said than done. I find coal dust in the oddest of places, even after spending weeks back in Liverpool. It's really quite insidious."

"Here we are." Bill pointed to a service corridor. "With this we can sneak right up on that first-class suite and they won't even know we're there."

"Not bad. I had no idea this was here."

"Bet you couldn't find your way back without help—it took me weeks to figure it all out."

"Bet I could. I have a photographic memory, you know."

Bill did know. It was one of those odd things about his brother. He could memorize virtually anything, with seemingly no effort. Had they been born of the aristocracy, he would undoubtedly have found his way to Oxford. As it was, he used his brawn far more than his brain. But being an avid reader, Avery actually enjoyed doing physical work that left his leisure time completely free. That way he could read whatever he chose without having to worry about coursework or job requirements. It's also why Bill periodically smuggled books to Avery from the extensive first-class library. As a steward, he had certain privileges that he was happy to share with his brother. The irony of it all was that Avery was probably better read than any of the young first-class passengers, even though they would certainly look down their noses at that burly fireman from below.

"Let's get on with it, then," said Avery. "I want to clean up as soon as I finish this job. I have a double shift off, and I don't want to waste it." The two brothers disappeared into the maze.

* * *

"Good evening, ladies and gentlemen. I hope you're having a pleasant crossing."

The men at the table stood up as a sign of respect for Captain Turner. "Thankfully a very uneventful crossing," said David Thomas, the coal magnate from Wales.

Turner nodded. "And you, ladies? I hope you are comfortable and well taken care of." A Mrs. Roberts responded quickly, her voice trembling and her face flushed. "Why, yes, Captain Turner. It's just wonderful! The food is marvelous and our room . . ."

Everett's mind wandered. It was a sign of social distinction to be seen with the captain of a ship, which is why so many passengers angled and maneuvered to be seated at his table. Of course, that honor was reserved for those who had the most expensive suites or who were the most famous, which is why it was so easy to flatter someone like Mrs. Roberts. She was carrying on and on in the mistaken belief that somehow it would matter to a luminary like the captain. Based on Everett's earlier conversation with Lord Baxter on the previous crossing, he realized that instead of impressing the captain, her prattle was undoubtedly driving him crazy.

"Yes, yes! Thank you. I'm glad that we're living up to your expectations." The exasperation in Turner's voice was obvious enough that everyone but dear Mrs. Roberts noticed. She blushed—not out of embarrassment, but rather for the recognition.

"Do you still have the same confidence about the crossing you expressed to the newspaper reporter in New York?" asked Everett. He didn't really care if the captain chose to see this as impertinent.

Turner looked at him directly and said, "Of course, the safety of our passengers is of paramount concern. But yes, I remain entirely confident that we shall have a safe and uneventful crossing." Before Everett could reply, Turner furrowed his brow. "We've met before, sir, but I'm afraid your name escapes me. I hope you'll forgive me for that."

"Stringham. Everett Stringham. I'm the coal mine owner from Wyoming. Sir William Baxter introduced us on our previous crossing from Liverpool to New York."

"Ah, yes. Baxter. He chewed me out on your behalf."

Everett's eyes widened. "On my behalf? But I expressed no problems. I thoroughly enjoyed my last voyage on the *Lusitania*."

"You're too kind. Sir William reminded me that I had promised you both a tour of the bridge, which I failed to provide. Perhaps I can remedy that on this crossing."

Everett nodded. "I was disappointed, of course, but I realized how busy you are. Still, it would be a great thrill for me."

"Perhaps tomorrow. I'll send an invitation to your room."

Everett tipped his head. "Thank you. I look forward to it."

"Well, then. I'll not interrupt your dinner any further. Please let us know if there's anything we can do to make your crossing more enjoyable. Ladies, my regards."

With that, the great Captain Turner, most senior captain in the Cunard pantheon, turned on his heel and moved straight toward the door of the first-class dining saloon. The fact that he failed to stop at any other table was seen by the Robertses as a sign that they were special and that their table had been singled out for recognition. It was viewed by Everett as a sign that the brief conversation at their table had been all that Captain Turner could stomach.

"That's a great honor to be invited to the bridge," said Mr. Roberts.

"Yes, I had no idea you were connected with Sir William," added Thomas.

"We met on my last crossing. A very genial fellow who seems perfectly at ease pressing Captain Turner. I have the sense that he's very much at home on a ship like this."

"Baxter is at home anywhere. You're fortunate to have him as a friend." Thomas gnawed on his unlit cigar. "Particularly in our line of work. You might put that to good advantage . . ." Thomas stopped the moment his wife slapped his wrist with her paper fan. "Oh, right—no talk of business at dinner." He smiled broadly to the others at the table. "Perhaps we can persuade Mr. Stringham to give us a report of what he finds up there on the bridge, given that we're all jealous of the invitation."

Chapter 15

To the Bottom of the Ocean

"Well?" Schweiger demanded. The captain of the small wooden schooner standing next to him looked miserable.

"Sir! No armaments or munitions found! Just a bunch of bacon, eggs, and potatoes," said the young German sailor Herman Lepper.

"Are you going to sink my little ship, anyway?"

"That was never in question. The only question was whether or not you and your crew would be on it when we fire on it." He was pleased to see the color drain from the man's face. "But, since you are not carrying articles of war, we will allow you and your crew to take to your lifeboat. But be quick about it. We do not like spending much time on the surface."

The man immediately made his way forward, ordering his stricken crew to lower the dilapidated lifeboat. The ship that Schweiger was about to sink, a 132-ton schooner named *Earl of Lathom,* had been spotted off the west coast of Ireland. The two-masted sailing ship, with the forward mast being shorter than the one behind it, was already a relic in the modern day of steam. It was a very small prize, but a prize nonetheless. Schweiger quickly returned to *U-20,* where he gave the order to use the deck gun to blast the wooden ship. The crew fired with relish, the first shell sending up a shower of wooden shrapnel. With a total of twelve shots, they successfully ripped the boat to shreds, sending it to the bottom in a matter of a few minutes. Schweiger watched as the crew of the schooner rowed forlornly toward the Irish coast, some ten miles distant.

"Very good, then," he said crisply. "It hardly makes up for our misfortune with that freighter, but at least it will send a chill up and down the Irish coast. They'll know we are here, and only the most intrepid will dare to venture out into the ocean."

"With all due respect, sir, it's hardly your fault that the torpedo misfired. It was clear that we hit the freighter. It was just cursed luck that it failed to explode."

Schweiger shook his head and responded to his pilot. "I doubt luck had anything to do with it, Lanz—neither good luck for them nor bad luck for us. It was shoddy manufacturing. Still, we are judged by the ships we sink, not by the number of torpedoes fired, and no one is interested in our excuses."

He scanned the horizon. "Let's take a chance and cruise on the surface for a while to put a full charge on the batteries. Perhaps the good news of this little sailboat is that our luck has finally turned."

"Aye, Captain!" Lanz passed the order down the voice pipe. By this point in the cruise, the thirty-two members of the *U-20* crew knew each other better than their own families. At 650 tons displacement, the *U-20* was a very cramped place for that many men to live. At 210 feet in length, but only 20 feet across, they literally lived on top of each other. The putrid smell of unwashed human bodies mingled with diesel oil fumes and cooking fires was overpowering, and the lack of privacy made any act of putting on pretense ridiculous. Fortunately, the crew trusted Schweiger implicitly and had great confidence in his ability to find worthy targets—the present kill of the schooner an exception, since it hadn't used up any of their precious torpedoes. The seven torpedoes—one now wasted—were the whole purpose of the cruise.

"Captain Schweiger!" said Lanz.

"Yes?"

"Out there, at ten o'clock—smoke on the horizon!"

Schweiger lifted his Zeiss binoculars to his eyes, scanning the horizon in the area indicated. "I think I see it," he said. Schweiger was self-confident enough that he had no trouble admitting that Lanz had superior skill in spotting and identifying enemy ships.

"Any idea what it is?"

Lanz didn't reply. Rather, he strained his eyes as he peered through his binoculars. "A steamer, I'd say. Roughly 3,000 tons." He waited a few moments longer. "She is Norweigan with neutral markings."

"I'm sure," replied Schweiger. "A neutral in these waters? Hardly. It's British, of that you can be sure. Just look at how high those neutral markings are—undoubtedly painted on tarpaulins that they've draped over her sides." Turning to the officer of the deck, he called out, "Submerge and prepare for an attack!" The order was passed down to the men below, and the deck crew quickly made their way inside the conning tower, pulling the watertight door behind them.

Schweiger moved confidently to the periscope, waiting for the ship to stabilize as it came to an even keel beneath the surface.

"Mark!" That was a command for the firing control officer to note the position of the periscope, which provided the initial calculation for the bearing the torpedo should be set to. Because the torpedo had no steering mechanism of its own, the attitude of the submarine itself was the key to its success. Stated another way, the submarine was like the barrel of a rifle with the torpedo acting the role of the shell. To aim the torpedo, the captain had to first aim the ship.

Schweiger updated the plot a few more times as the distance between the submarine and its prey shortened. "Take a look, Lanz."

Lanz moved quickly into position and peered through the periscope. The lighting at this time of the day was tricky, so it was difficult to be sure. Finally he confirmed the captain's firing solution. At just 275 meters, it should be an easy shot but still precarious, given the speed of the freighter. Because both the target and the torpedo were moving in the water at the same time, the trick was to fire ahead of the advancing target so that it would sail into the path of the torpedo. Schweiger moved quickly back to the periscope. "Fire!"

Lanz clicked the stopwatch, and they counted off the time. Schweiger cursed. "They started a turn just as we were firing." The crew on the bridge strained even more carefully to hear what Schweiger had to say next, as if through their own concentration they could will the torpedo to hit the target. Lanz was first to know the answer as the seconds ticked away with no explosion. "A miss," he said dejectedly.

Schweiger backed away from the periscope. "Mr. Lanz is correct. The torpedo passed in front of the ship. A miss, and now they have turned on a course that is impossible for us to match. Our nine knots submerged can never close the gap." The disappointment in the room was palpable, although no one would be so impudent as to say anything.

"Come hard about! We need to get out of here." The danger now was that the freighter would use its wireless transmitter to send a distress signal, and any British warships in the area would come racing to the spot to attack the *U-20.* The crew immediately undertook the task of turning the various valves that would make it possible to implement the captain's command. "Mr. Rikowski, once we're clear we'll surface and report our position. The fog is closing in again, and soon we'll be safely hidden from any other British warships." Otto Rikowski was the radio operator. With this new order, he moved quickly to the radio set in order to start the tubes warming up.

"A disappointment," said Schweiger, "but there will be other opportunities."

* * *

"MAY I BE OF ASSISTANCE?" asked Everett Stringham of the young woman who was in the process of showing a group of children how to put on their life jackets.

"Why, yes, thank you. Perhaps you could help this little fellow. His mother has two others to keep her busy." Everett smiled and leaned down to show an older boy of perhaps twelve years how to tighten the life jacket around his slender body.

"I'm surprised to see you leading this exercise," Everett said genially.

"The crew isn't providing any instruction," replied the young woman with disdain. He had earlier learned that she was a passenger in the second-class cabins, even though she was now helping young families from steerage. "They know we're going into the war zone, and yet they leave us completely unprepared." She shook her head in annoyance.

"There you go!" said Everett to the boy. "Tied perfectly. Not that you'll ever need it, but it's always wise to be prepared." The boy joined his family, and the mother thanked the woman conducting the exercise and then pushed her children along to return to their cramped cabin below.

"Thank you," said the young woman. "You're a real life saver." She smiled at the unintended pun.

"I really can't believe the crew isn't doing this. The printed instructions on the inside of the cabin doors are hardly sufficient."

"I agree," she said. "It was with the greatest reluctance that Captain Turner gave our committee permission to do even this. He said he didn't want us to alarm the passengers nor to suggest that this basic safety measure is important. I think he worries about a panic. But if we did have an emergency—even one unrelated to the Germans—he'd see genuine panic if people don't know something as simple as to how to put on a life jacket."

Everett nodded in agreement. "Well, if you don't need me anymore, I think I'll go back to my cabin and check on my own life jacket." She smiled and thanked him again.

* * *

May 6, 1915—Near the Coningbeg Lightship Off the Waterford Coast

"Make full speed. Deck crew, prepare to fire!"

"You're not going to submerge?" asked Lanz.

"With this much fog, there's little risk of us being fired on or rammed. Let's save our torpedoes."

"Ah, this is a fun one . . ."

"Fun for the hound, not so much for the fox," replied Schweiger. "They're going to make a run for the fog! Be quick about it!" The gun crew responded instantly, quickly signalling they were ready.

"No name and no flag," said Lanz cautiously. "She may really be a neutral."

"If there's the slightest question, we must attack. In this case a neutral should display both her flag and her markings. Otherwise I have to conclude the ship is British or running contraband."

With that, Schweiger ordered the gun crew to open fire. The gun crew cheered when Schweiger confirmed two direct hits, but the steamer continued at full speed into the fog bank.

"Maintain top speed, current course." Schweiger was not going to give up so easily. After a few minutes of plowing through the mist, they spotted the huge ship through a brief break in the cover. "Shoot at will!" As shell after shell pounded into the relative giant of a ship, it finally slowed to a halt. Without any overt order from Schweiger, the crew of the stricken tanker started abandoning ship as they made their way into four tiny lifeboats. Unfortunately, one of these little boats turned turtle in the water, leaving the crew swimming anxiously.

"They'll be all right. As close as we are to shore, there will be rescue ships in no time." Schweiger looked around nervously. "Which is why we have to put an end to her." Leaning down to the speaking tube he gave the order to fire one of their bronze torpedoes directly into the engine room. They were close enough that the deck crew could see the progress of the torpedo right up until it smashed into the side of the freighter, sending up a great plume of water and smoke. Now they waited expectantly for the inevitable gurgling plunge to the bottom. But somehow the obstinate ship managed to maintain its profile in the water.

"Why won't that cursed ship sink?" asked Lanz.

"We have to take care of this. Ahead slow!"

"What are you going to do?"

"I'm going to have the crew shoot her below the waterline." After working *U-20* very close to the freighter, the command was given and the shots fired. Now the results were immediately apparent, and the ship started down.

"Can you identify the ship?"

Lanz said, "I'm quite certain it's the *Candidate,* a 6,000-ton Liverpool steamer."

"So it is British, after all."

"I'm certain of it."

Schweiger smiled. "A clean kill. Let's see what else is out there waiting for us."

* * *

IT DIDN'T TAKE LONG TO find out what was waiting. In less than an hour, they spotted a marvelous prize—a 16,000-ton passenger steamer with no visible markings. "A ship of the White Star Line," Schweiger had properly guessed. But his attempts to maneuver into position to get off a good clean bow shot failed because of the speed of the ship, the *Arabic,* which sped past them at 10,000 feet away. That was way too far to launch a torpedo.

"Ah, well. Let's dive, gentlemen, and get some respite from all this fog. We'll lie in wait and see what the ocean brings us."

An hour later, Schweiger gave the order to come up to thirty-six feet, where he found that the fog had cleared. As the clock ticked past noon, the word was received "heave in sight," with smoke barreling up into the sky.

"We have a much better position this time." He peered through the periscope again. "In fact, she's going to pass right by our nose!" When the enemy vessel reached just 250 meters, he gave the order to launch one of the more expensive gyro torpedoes, which was supposed to provide much greater accuracy than the older bronze. Fortunately, in this case it did just that.

"A direct hit!" Schweiger called out, to the joy of the crew. They immediately felt the concussion as it rumbled past them in the water. "A hit near the bridge . . . the ship is already sinking."

"Voegele!" Schweiger called out to the young electrician who had been drafted a short time earlier. "It's your turn to see through the periscope." U-boat captains had learned early on that it was a great boost to morale to allow the young men of the crew to take turns looking through the periscope. Nearly all the crewmen were young—Schweiger, for example, had been made a U-boat captain just a year earlier, at the ripe old age of twenty-seven. Looking through the periscope often relieved the terror some felt as they crawled blindly through the darkness of the depths. When fully submerged, the crew could see absolutely no light, even through the small portholes in the conning tower. But at thirty-six feet, you could see the outside world through the mirrors and lenses of the periscope.

"Thank you, sir." Voegele stepped forward tentatively. As he gazed through the lens, a broad smile broke out on his face. "I can see! I can see it!" Lanz chuckled quietly, inasmuch as that's what they all said when first peering through the scope. But as Voegele started to describe the scene for the others in the control room, his voice suddenly tightened, and he hesitated. Schweiger leaned forward to observe him.

"Are you all right, Voegele?"

The young man half stumbled as he withdrew. "Yes, sir," he stammered. "I'm fine."

It was very odd behavior at such a moment of triumph, so Schweiger stepped back to the periscope to see what was happening. As he looked through the lens, he saw the chaos of men jumping from the burning ship into the water. Some of the enemy sailors were on fire themselves, undoubtedly desperate to extinguish the flames in the water. Of course, they weren't thinking of the fact that as soon as the salt water found their burns, the agony would be even more excruciating. As he moved the scope slightly, he saw an overturned boat with men clinging desperately to its sides, all the while looking in the direction of the submarine to see if it was going to surface and fire on them.

"Ah, Voegele. That is what this is about. They are our enemies, and the only way to save our homeland is to do things just like this."

"Yes, sir. Of course." Voegele's breathing was labored and desperate. "Of course, I understand."

Schweiger nodded, although Voegele's behavior was disturbing. "The lifeboats have cleared. We'll fire one of our bronze torpedoes to make certain the ship goes down. It's at least 6,000 tons, and I'm certain that it's English. Take a look, Lanz."

Lanz looked and offered his informed guess that it was the *Centurion,* operated by the same company that owned the *Candidate.*

As the second torpedo slammed into the ship, Schweiger confirmed the damage visually, although the noise coming through the water was more than enough to confirm that the ship was doomed. "All right, then, let's move out to sea and consider our options. We have three torpedoes left. One for some other ship and two to get us home safely." He looked up and smiled at his crew. Schweiger was at ease in a leadership role. He was also ruthlessly cool in shooting at enemies, as evidenced by his attack on the hospital ship. At least there was no second-guessing about this ship. Casting a glance to Voegele, he called out to the crew, "A very successful day, indeed! A draught of good German beer for everyone while we decide what course to follow." Of course, that brought a cheer and many congratulations to Schweiger as he retired to his tiny cabin.

* * *

EVERETT STRINGHAM WAS ENJOYING THE benefit concert immeasurably when Captain Turner came into the room. This was the last social event of the voyage, the Passengers' Talent Concert, which was a fundraiser for the Seamans' Charity, and they had so far been graced by singers, piano players, and even amateur comedians. Some were great successes, others an embarrassment, but it was all for a good cause. The emcee raised his arm and reached out toward the captain. "And now, ladies and gentlemen, I see that we are favored by the presence of Captain Turner, the most celebrated captain of all the great ocean liners on the seas. The trials he has endured and the men he has saved are the stuff of legends. Captain Turner, I hope you'll take a moment to address us?"

Turner nodded, although he wasn't smiling. "Good evening, ladies and gentlemen. I'm sorry to interrupt this marvelous concert in which our guests show off their talents. I'm sure it is the equal of Broadway and the West End. Is that true, Mr. Frohman?"

Charles Frohman smiled. "I've been thinking of canceling my engagements in London and simply offering contracts to everyone who has performed here tonight. They would light up Broadway for the next year." The amateurs in the show blushed, and the professionals who had graced the group with their more polished talents smiled at Frohman's satirical flourish.

"Yes, well, that's good. On a more serious note, it seems we've received warning of submarines in the area." He raised his hands as some of the guests gasped. "But there is no cause for alarm. Tomorrow we shall come under the protection of the Royal Navy. You can be assured that we will steam at full speed so as to arrive in Liverpool in good time."

"Are you taking any precautions?" someone asked.

"We've been cautious the entire voyage, of course. But I would like you all to draw your curtains tonight so that no lights show through. I would also ask the gentlemen to refrain from lighting their cigarettes on deck; we don't want to draw attention to ourselves. Aside from that, we have prepared the lifeboats and all other commonsense measures." He did his best to smile—not a natural act for Turner—and concluded. "But there really is nothing to fear."

As he started through the crowd, he was stopped by none other than Alfred Vanderbilt. "A question, Captain Turner?"

Turner pulled up and turned, clearly annoyed at the interruption. "Of course, Mr. Vanderbilt."

"Our progress has been unusually slow. Try as I might to win the daily pool for number of miles traveled, I haven't been able to guess a number low enough. Can you answer me why it is that we're making such painfully slow progress? And what does this leisurely pace mean now that we've entered the war zone?"

Turner drew himself up, and the crowd braced for his reply. Turner was not used to being challenged.

"We have been ordered to conserve coal, Mr. Vanderbilt. There is a war on."

"And so we are placed in greater peril, even though we paid full fare?"

"Not in the least. Should the need arise, we are capable of twenty-two knots. And this speed is far greater than any German U-boat's. If a submarine happened to spot us, they would never have time to maneuver into position to attack before we were long since beyond them."

"But you do not intend to sail at that speed unless some unusual event intervenes. So the fact remains that we have been steaming at an incredibly low rate. I must say that I am annoyed by this. I am friends with the chairman of Cunard, you know, and fear that I will have to make him aware of this decision of yours."

Turner tipped his head back and noticeably bit his lip. Before responding, he took a deep breath. "I think that's a very reasonable thing to do, Mr. Vanderbilt. After all, it is *he* who issued the order, so I'm sure he'll be prepared to discuss it with you. In the meantime, I am left to follow my orders."

Vanderbilt was taken aback by this and chose not to reply. Turner returned his gaze to the crowd. "Again, you have nothing to worry about. Now I hope you'll have an enjoyable evening." He departed quickly before anyone could ask another question.

"It will be a little harder to have a good evening after that announcement," said Everett to David Thomas. "Submarines in the area, boilers shut down. It does seem a bit ominous."

"Very distressing," Thomas agreed. Everett waited for the famous British resolve which was certain to follow. Thomas pursed his lips. "Still, we have to trust the Admiralty. We are in the war zone, and they certainly know we are coming. I'll take my comfort in that."

* * *

"Shafer!"

Bill jumped at the sound of John Todd's voice. Thus far on the voyage, Todd had pretty well ignored him.

"Sir?"

Todd came down the hall tentatively until he was perhaps three or four feet from Bill.

Todd cleared his throat. "I just wanted to thank you . . . for your brother's help. It was a great service to us, and I've put him in for a commendation."

Bill let his breath out. "Thank you, sir. I'm sure he'll be very pleased by that."

He wanted to add how much Avery hoped to become an engineer, but somehow that seemed superfluous.

"Yes, well, it was . . . good of you to arrange it."

Bill nodded. It felt as if Todd wanted to say more and was simply using this as an excuse.

"Is everything in order with your guests?"

"Everything seems in good order. They seem far more nervous than usual, but perhaps that's to be expected."

"Indeed it is. We have to help them stay calm. The way to do that is for those of us in service to act calm."

"Of course."

Todd took a deep breath and let it out slowly. "Well, I'll release you to your duties, then."

Todd turned and disappeared down the corridor. Bill leaned against the wall and closed his eyes. He didn't know which was worse—the arrogant Todd who was a firm leader or the gentler Todd who was so tentative. At least he wasn't in trouble. He was glad of that.

CHAPTER 16
THE WAR ZONE

May 7, 1915 —Near the Southwest Coast of Ireland

"WELCOME TO THE BRIDGE, MR. STRINGHAM. Captain Turner has asked me to be your host."

Everett smiled in anticipation—probably in the very same way that an eight-year-old would smile if invited to tour a candy factory. But he couldn't help himself. Here was the command and control center of the entire ship, all 44,000 tons of her. The decisions made here affected all of them. Stepping across the threshold, he stepped into the immaculately appointed bridge. Like all modern ships, it was fully enclosed with the officers looking out through broad windows at the front and sides. The walls were painted a dazzling white, the floor made of highly polished wooden planks, and everything else was brass, or so it seemed.

"We'll stay behind the officers on duty so as to not distract them."

Everett assumed he was being taken around by a junior officer, given the young man's age and appearance, but he had no idea how to identify the rank of people in the merchant service.

"As you can see forward, we have the wheel, which allows the helmsman to control the rudder."

Everett nodded, since that's the one thing that everyone expects to find on a bridge. "It's smaller than I expected. Somehow I visualized a wheel the size of those on a sailing ship or perhaps on a Mississippi steamboat. I had the good fortune to visit the wheelhouse of one many years ago."

"Those wheels are much larger, since they are connected mechanically to the rudder. A person needs a great deal of leverage to execute the captain's orders. The *Lusitania* is connected electrically, so the real work of steering the ship is done by electric motors and steam. You might be surprised to know that the rudder weighs somewhat more than a hundred tons."

Everett whistled. Only 200,000 pounds of finely tapered steel to change the direction of such a massive ship.

"Of course, the rudder is only one element of the steering, since a great deal of maneuvering can be controlled by use of the multiple propellers." Pointing to a gleaming brass instrument to the right of the wheel, he explained, "The captain uses these repeaters to control the turning of the screws. If he needs to make an unusually tight turn, such as when we're maneuvering through a harbor, he can reverse the turbines on, say, the port screw, while giving forward thrust on the starboard side. That will swing the ship smartly to port. It's particularly effective when traveling at slow speeds."

Everett ached to go touch one of the gleaming brass repeaters, which were floor-mounted telegraphs with a large dial on each side whereon was printed AHEAD FULL, STOP, and FULL REVERSE, with gradations in between.

"It's all right," said the young man, motioning Everett to step forward so he could see. "When the officer of the deck gives an order to change the speed of one of the engines, he pushes the handles all the way forward to synchronize the pointer on our dial up here with the dial on an identical telegraph down in the engine room. He then pulls the levers back to the new desired speed. This new speed is repeated to the engine room. When the chief engineer sees and hears the change, he confirms it by moving his own dials to the new setting. His actions are repeated up here so we know he received the order and will execute it—hence the name "repeaters."

Everett nodded. Of course, he had used technology extensively in his coal mines—something this young man could not know—but still it was fascinating to see how innovatively engineers had solved the problem of instantly conveying orders from the bridge to the engine room in such a massive ship as this.

"Why don't you use telephones?"

"A good question. Telephones are fairly new and not entirely reliable. Besides, the noise in the engine room can be distracting. With the repeaters, there is no question of what is desired, thus reducing the chance of an error."

Everett nodded. Of course, it made sense.

"You can see there are repeaters for each of the engines. In most instances, the same command will be given for all engines, unless we're carrying out an intricate order, such as the hypothetical one I described earlier."

"Very fascinating."

The young man then walked him toward the back of the bridge. "This panel controls all the watertight doors in the ship. In the event of a fire or a flood, the captain can immediately close the appropriate doors to isolate the area in danger from the rest of the ship."

The miracle of electricity was still new enough that it somehow seemed magical. By manipulating some hand-sized controls here in the bridge, huge motors or hydraulics would activate in remote places on the ship, perhaps saving all on board.

"Finally, let me show you how we plot our progress." They walked to a map table where the navigator was busy drawing lines on a complex map, which was hardly recognizable because of all the small numbers printed on it. "These numbers represent the depth of the ocean floor. We have maps that take us all the way across the Atlantic. It's of far greater concern when we come close to land, since there are small islands and outcrops that could damage the ship if we didn't have a precise plot."

"And how do you accomplish that?"

The navigator looked up and responded. "We have all the tools that have been available for centuries to take celestial bearings. We can be very accurate when that's available, but when there's fog, like this morning, those tools are useless. Fortunately, we have identifiable landmarks that allow us to plot our location precisely when we're near land. We then use dead reckoning to keep an approximate plot until we can take a more accurate reading. I'm sure Captain Turner will want us to get a very accurate reading as we draw closer to Ireland, so he's confident of our navigation as we enter the Irish Sea."

Everett expressed thanks for this explanation, and then the young officer pointed out the captain's bridge cabin—a small alcove at the back of the bridge where he could lie down to nap if he needed to stay close to the bridge. When Everett asked if that was standard on passenger ships, the young man replied that it was not but that the *Lusitania* had been built with government assistance so that it could be converted to military use if needed. Thus, the bridge was a hybrid of merchant ship and military.

"Please convey my deep appreciation to the captain. This has been a remarkable experience, and I have even greater admiration for the work you gentlemen do than before."

The officer tipped his hand to his hat and escorted Everett to the door.

As he made his way down to his cabin, Everett was surprised to find Bill working there. "I just returned from the bridge."

"Really? I've never been up there. Is it impressive?"

Everett smiled. "Very. Although quite austere, really—virtually no adornment, and I was surprised at how few actual controls and valves and such things there are. I learned that the real controls are largely dispersed throughout the ship to be activated by orders from the bridge."

"I'm glad you told me. I'd probably never have known otherwise." Bill straightened up. "I'll be out of your way, then."

Everett stepped partially forward. "Bill . . ."

"Sir?"

Everett cleared his throat. "It's just that we should make it into port tonight, and then I'm taking a train directly to London. I'm not sure we'll have a chance to talk again."

Bill nodded. "I guess that's right. I hadn't really thought about it. I've been mostly worried about how to tell Mum that I want to enlist in the navy."

"Well, I was just wondering . . . so much has happened in the past weeks."

"You were wondering what I think about all of it?" Everett nodded. "I had a great time with you and Mrs. Stringham. And I very much liked Elder Carlson. The things that Mr. Todd said about his sister bother me, but it seems that you helped him feel better about it." Bill paused for a moment. "I guess I know I don't know enough to judge. I've decided to surprise Mum by asking her to take me to church when I get home. Perhaps one day I'll know as much as you and Elder Carlson. Until then, I won't close it out."

Everett smiled. "I'm glad. For our part, we loved having you along. It helped me miss my own son and daughter less. Thank you for spending the weekend with us."

"Of course."

"And for that little matter of saving my life."

Bill smiled and then departed.

* * *

"CURSE THIS FOG. WE'RE RUNNING out of time, and we still have three torpedoes. It would be shameful to return to Germany with so little success."

Lanz acknowledged the captain's frustration. And so far, May 7 had produced no targets, even though they were lying in wait right off the Irish coast on a route frequented by steamers and troopships.

But Schweiger was not one to brood. "Prepare to surface!" His voice exuded confidence. More quietly to Lanz, he said, "Let's give it one more try."

As *U-20* breached the surface, the deck crew made its way up the ladder, while Schweiger lingered below. Then he received a breathless call to the bridge from one of the watch. Flying up the rungs of the metal ladder, he stepped out onto the deck and immediately raised his glasses in the direction the watchman was pointing.

In an astonished voice, the captain said, "There are so many masts and funnels. Two or three ships." He continued to study the image in his binoculars. "No. No, it's a single ship. A ship with *four* masts!"

He pulled his eyes back from the binoculars and rubbed them. "Four. There are distinctly four funnels! Prepare to dive! Prepare to dive!"

As he slid down the steel railings on each side of the ladder, he called out to the crew, "Four funnels, schooner rig, upward of 25,000 tons! Speed about twenty-two knots. It's heading right for us. It's probably too much to hope she'll hold this course, but the next hour will tell." Schweiger licked his lips in anticipation. He marked the time at 13:20.

Chapter 17
Torpedo Running

After maneuvering at nine knots for more than an hour underwater, the *U-20* had closed to within two miles of the massive four-funnel ship, which was advancing at approximately eighteen to twenty knots. Just when it seemed success was possible, the great ship had changed course.

"Curse them!" Schweiger had shouted. "They've turned away." To launch at that point would have been to waste a torpedo, since even at the ridiculously slow speed the great liner was traveling, there was no way the weapon could reach the ship.

Schweiger had turned away from the periscope for a moment, resigned to the disappointment of fate. As he did so, he invited his pilot to come take a look. Before Lanz arrived, Schweiger decided to take one last look. When he did, he let out an audible gasp.

"Wait a minute! They have turned toward us again. They are coming directly into our sights!"

"Is the ship zigzagging?" asked Lanz.

Schweiger shook his head in disbelief. "Straight and steady." He looked up again. "She could not be sailing a more perfect course if her captain had deliberately decided to give us a dead-on shot." Turning to Voegele at the voice tube, the captain gave the order for his torpedo officer, Raimund Weisbach, to prepare to fire a G-torpedo, the fifth of seven.

"Hydroplanes and rudder are set to a depth of ten feet," Weisbach confirmed.

"Is it a troopship or a passenger ship?"

Schweiger turned to Voegele, the young electrician on his first cruise. "And what difference does that make?" He was disgusted by the look of concern on the young man's face. "Now prepare to relay my order."

Schweiger waited until the distance between the two ships had narrowed to just five hundred feet. "Shoot!" he shouted.

But nothing happened.

Raising his eyes from the periscope, he looked around to see what had interfered with his order. Voegele looked back at him with anxious eyes. "But if it's a passenger ship, there will be women and children!"

Schweiger swore at him and bellowed, "Shoot, blast you, shoot!"

When Voegele still hesitated, pilot Lanz shoved him out of the way and shouted the order into the voice tube. All on board were at first mesmerized by this drama, almost holding their breath until they could feel a shudder and hear the hiss of escaping air as the torpedo rocketed from its tube. If any other member of the crew beside Voegele felt any qualms about firing on a passenger ship, no man revealed it.

"Torpedo running!" said Schweiger as he watched the trail of bubbles through the periscope, now sailing through the water in a perfect line to hit the great behemoth amidships.

"Gott strafe England!"

* * *

"THIS MAKES NO SENSE!"

Everett and David Thomas couldn't help but overhear a fellow first-class passenger talking loudly with one of the officers. The passenger was some kind of a shipping magnate who knew the ocean well.

"But it does, Mr. Perlman. The fog has been heavy, and this break in the weather allows the captain to finally get a firm bearing. It's crucial that we fix our position precisely so that we can time our arrival at Liverpool. If we're off, we could be forced to stand outside the Mersey Bar lightship throughout the entire night until the tide is again favorable, and that exposes us to a great deal of risk. Better to time our approach deliberately, and now that we have Ireland in site, we can get our bearings."

"But why so slow? It feels as if we're crawling."

The officer was agitated, and it was obvious that it was difficult for him to continue the argument in this fashion. "We're going eighteen knots while the captain takes a four-point bearing. It's the most accurate possible reading to take."

"Four-points!" Perlman was incredulous. "That will take at least twenty minutes on a rock-solid steady course. You couldn't give the Germans a more precise target. Certainly a two-point would be sufficient—and it would take only five minutes!"

The officer straightened. "I've told you more than I should have, Mr. Perlman. There is no finer captain on the seas than Captain Turner, and I'm sure he has his reasons. Good day, sir!"

Perlman shook his head in disbelief, which was perceived by Thomas and Everett as an opening for them to join him. "What does it mean—a four-point bearing?" asked Everett.

"In normal circumstances it would be a reasonable thing to do—it's the most accurate bearing that can be taken, since you sight in on four distinct points of land. But in most instances, it is way more than is needed, since a two- or three-point bearing is very nearly as accurate and is much quicker to take. Given the dangers in these waters, a two- or three-point bearing should be more than adequate. The problem right now is that we have to hold our course absolutely steady while the bearings are being taken."

They wandered over to the starboard railing, toward the stern of the ship. With the ship heading east toward England, the coast of Ireland was now off the port side, approximately ten miles to the north. The fog had lifted just a short time ago, and now the day was brilliant. Looking off to starboard, they could see the open ocean glistening in the sun.

"A fine lunch," said Everett, in an attempt to break the tension, having just come from the first-class dining room.

"I'll be glad when this voyage is over," replied David Thomas.

"And then I'll feel foolish for shouting at that officer, I am sure," said Perlman. "But for all the anxiety displayed in the press about this cruise, the captain acts as if there is nothing to be concerned about. I wish I was as settled as he is." Perlman looked around. "And just where are the British warships that we were promised? We're sitting here as exposed as a naked baby playing near an alligator pit . . . and not a destroyer or cruiser to be seen. Why is it that more people aren't as distressed as I am?"

"You Americans will never fully understand," said Thomas. "In Britain we made the decision centuries ago that we all fit into a certain class, and we will never question what those in a superior class have decided to do. Their lordships at the Admiralty have their reasons, and they must be right—that's just the way it is. It's how our society copes with uncertainty."

Everett was about to say something when they heard shouting farther forward on the ship. As they turned to see what the commotion was about, they noticed dozens of passengers streaming toward the rail, pointing out to sea and shouting.

"What is it?" asked Perlman anxiously.

"There!" said Everett. "Look there—in the water. It's a track—a torpedo! I'm sure of it!"

"It *is* a track!" said Perlman. "We are all dead for sure!"

Everett and Perlman were two of the few to shout. It was as if the several hundred passengers watching the approaching torpedo from the various railings of the ship were mesmerized. Those who were standing above the place where it was about to strike should have been running for their lives, but instead they just stood there, transfixed. It was one of those moments when time seemed to stand still, and yet the torpedo was upon them before they could even acknowledge its reality.

It was real, though, as was amply proved when the line of bubbles intersected the *Lusitania*'s line of travel just behind the bridge. There was a terrific concussion as a giant waterspout shot up into the air. Adding to the shock wave of the explosion was the sickening sound of twisting steel and shattering glass as the side of the ship below the waterline was blasted into a twisting wreck of jagged shrapnel.

Everett, Thomas, and Perlman were far enough back that they weren't directly impacted by the blast, but they were certainly stunned by it. As the sound of the explosion subsided, Everett recovered his footing just before a second blast—perhaps even more powerful than the first—rocked the ship. This time it appeared as if the entire side of the ship was blown out into the water.

"We've got to get our life jackets!" shouted Thomas. "There's no way the ship can stand that kind of abuse and stay afloat for long." The desperate look in his eyes was all the more gruesome because of the blood that rained down on them as the water and fragments of bodies thrown up by the waterspout cascaded down around them.

Everett knew that Thomas was right, although he'd heard that it would take more than an hour for the ship to actually sink—if it really did sink. The *Lusitania* would be far more likely to founder until the passengers were off, and then the German U-boat would sink it with another torpedo.

"I said we should get to our life jackets!" Thomas screamed.

"I know!" replied Everett. Try as he might, Everett could not make himself move. That problem was solved rather quickly when Perlman blasted his way between the two men, knocking Everett to the deck. Everett winced as he fell on his injured arm. A searing wave of pain shot up his arm as he heard it crack, perhaps breaking in the same place again. The shock of the fall was enough that he was instantly furious with Perlman, and he looked up to see where the man was going so he could yell at him. Everett could see the man was going nowhere in particular. In a surreal fashion, Perlman ran forward, turned back and ran toward them, turned, and then ran toward the port side of the ship. The look on his face was unnerving—sheer panic disfiguring his features.

Perlman was the exception. The vast majority of the crowd who had actually witnessed the blast without being killed by its impact was simply standing there benumbed. Everett understood their inaction. It was shock. Shock and uncertainty of what to do next.

"Let me help you up, Stringham." Everett looked up and nodded appreciatively as Thomas kneeled down next to him and put his arms under Everett's good shoulder to raise him up.

"Thank you," said Everett quietly. It took a couple of tries to make any sound come out.

"Yes, well. I really have to leave you to yourself. I need to find my wife and daughter."

"Of course you do."

Thomas looked at him and held his gaze for just a moment. "Will you be all right, Stringham?"

Everett nodded. The shock of a few moments ago was quickly being replaced by a knot in his stomach as he realized that with his injured arm and bruised ribs, he was now a liability—a handicapped person who would have a hard time contributing to any rescue. "Yes, I'm all right. Please go find your family."

Thomas nodded. But he hesitated one more moment. "Good luck, Stringham. If I don't see you again . . ."

Everett nodded. There really was nothing more to be said.

Thomas went running off toward the door into the superstructure of the ship. At this point people had finally started to react—the beginning of a mass panic.

Everett started to stumble his way toward the deck door. He was sure it was his imagination, but it already felt as if the ship was listing to starboard. While that made no logical sense, the physical impact of the explosion made anything seem possible. Everett felt a wave of panic come over him. As he made it to the first-class elevator, he was greeted by a panicked crowd that was trying to force its way onto the elevator. Men were shoving women, babies were crying, and the whole melee was chaotic.

"That won't work," he said to himself, so he made his way to the stairway. By now the pain in his arm was excruciating, and the jarring of each and every step caused him to wince. In spite of that, he forced himself to go on. Finally making it to his deck, he struggled toward his cabin. Surprisingly, he was alone at this point, which made it easier to hear the groaning of the metal as the ship settled in ways that its builders had never contemplated. Every so often the air was punctured by the sound of something crashing or smashing somewhere below. Even the lights flickered, went out, and then came back on.

When Everett finally made it to his cabin, he struggled with the key. With one useless arm it was very difficult to do anything intricate, particularly since the ship was unsteady under his feet. It was obviously slowing but also listing as it went, which made it extremely unstable. "There!" he shouted to himself, as the key finally turned. With sweat dripping down his face, he swung the door open at exactly the same moment that the ship lurched violently. He was thrown against the door, his injured arm the point of contact. The pain was searing, more than anything he'd ever experienced, and as he recoiled from the door, he felt himself falling toward the floor. In spite of his better instincts, he couldn't stop himself from thrusting both arms out to catch himself. When his injured arm collided with the floor, the pain was simply unbearable and Everett Stringham passed out—unconscious and alone on a sinking ship.

* * *

AVERY SHAFER STUMBLED IN THE dark, absolutely terrified. One moment he'd been shoveling a load of coal deep inside his boiler, and the next moment the world exploded around him. Although his brain registered the awful sound of metal being torn asunder, he could hear nothing now but an overwhelming ringing in his ears, and his side hurt. The blast had thrown him against the side of the furnace behind his assigned station. In the orange glow of the fires that were now burning out of control all around him, he could see men shouting but couldn't hear a word they were saying. He didn't need to, really. It was easy enough to make out the word *torpedo* as people shouted, apparently at the top of their lungs.

"Get out!"

Avery jumped at the touch of his supervisor, who had somehow come up from behind him. "GET OUT, SHAFER—ANY WAY YOU CAN!" He knew the man was shouting, but he barely heard the words.

Nodding quickly, he clung to his shovel and started making his way toward what had been the usual exit. The boilers were centered on the deck, and there was room to pass down rows between them—that was one way. The other was to go to the outside edge near the bulkheads where the coal was stored. As he felt the ice-cold water of the Atlantic come up around his feet, the hair on the back of his neck stood up, and he knew that he didn't want to go anywhere near the hull. He needed as much time as possible. So he made his way toward the center, and then, acting on pure instinct, he turned aft, somehow sensing the tilt to the deck that told him the blast had been forward of his position and that he needed to go toward the back of the ship. To go forward, which was his usual exit, would take him directly to the torpedo breach.

Electric lighting in the boiler rooms was always dim at best because of the coal dust. Now it was downright infernal—the light of a hundred fires burning all around him. Some of the furnaces had cracked open, with the fires inside fully visible, the metal glowing white hot. Other furnaces had spewed their burning coal from the open doors where it had ignited the piles of coal waiting to be fed into the furnaces. But as ominous as it was to be surrounded by flames, it was even worse when he cast a glance behind him to see the fires going out one by one as water poured over the chunks of burning coal, extinguishing them as it progressed.

As he started running, Avery was surprised he could move at all. When the blast hit the ship, the compression of the air inside the sealed chamber of the hull had knocked him right off his feet, throwing him against the wall of the boiler behind him. As he stumbled along, he felt a stabbing side ache on his right side, even though he hadn't been running very long.

"Avery! Avery Shafer!" His hearing must not have been entirely gone, because he did faintly hear the voice of his friend Jake Patterson. It was the most thrilling thing he'd ever heard.

Spinning around, he shouted, "Jake! Jake! You're alive."

"We've got to go this way, Avery." Patterson was pointing in the direction of the huge service elevator that was used to bring coal and supplies down into the ship's bowels. Avery nodded and started following Patterson. But as they drew near the elevator, they could see that it was already crowded with men. "There's room, come with me." Jake tried to drag him along, but Avery instinctively shook himself loose from Jake's grasp.

"No! We should NOT take the elevator!"

"What? Are you crazy? We've got to get out of here."

Avery shook his head. "I'm not going."

Jake shook his head and cursed but let go of Avery and ran for the elevator, just as the operator pulled the screen closed. *Why did you do that?* Avery asked himself. *Idiot!* With escape that close at hand, he'd refused it. While it made no sense, he'd had the definite impression not to get on the elevator. Now he knew he needed to find his way to a stairwell, and fast. The water was up around his calves and rising.

Out of the blue, a terrific shrieking noise assaulted his slowly recovering ears, followed by a wave of scalding steam that singed the back of his head and sent him tumbling face-first into the water on the floor. He flailed in the water while inhaling filthy coal water. Spluttering, he crouched up to a sitting position just as the lights went out. A boiler must have exploded, he reasoned. He found it odd that he could be so rational and so absolutely panicked at the same moment.

The explosion made sense. The inside of each boiler was filled with superheated steam. When the ice-cold water of the ocean hit the metal, it was only natural that a reaction would occur. The exploded boiler hadn't withstood the change in temperature. Regardless of the cause, the lights were out, and now all he had to guide him was his own knowledge of the ship and the emergency lights that flared dimly above him.

Gotta keep moving, Avery. As he looked behind him, he could see that only a handful of men were still alive after the explosion. Most had probably been killed by the pressure from the blast. Others were already drowning as they stumbled and fell into the water. Those who had been working in more forward compartments had very likely been killed by the sheer force of the water that was even now surging into the hull of the ship.

To calm himself as he moved through the gloom, he tried to figure out what had happened. It's not like he could do anything about it, but he had to do *something* to control his thinking. *We were hit by a torpedo. It blew a hole in the side of the ship. We were moving forward at approximately eighteen knots, according to my supervisor. But we were under full steam in case the captain needed full power. Now we've got water surging in through the breach because of our forward momentum. The bulkheads weren't fully sealed in time, and now the doors can't close because of the water pressure. That's why the water is chasing you. You've got to get past the next bulkhead, or you're going to be entombed in here.*

Panic and adrenaline flooded him. He guessed that he had about sixty seconds to make it to the next bulkhead, or he was doomed. His heart started racing as he forced himself to run in a crouch; there was less dust closer to the ground, so he could see more clearly and breathe easier.

"You've gotta get to that bulkhead!" he yelled at himself. But to do so, he had to push through the pain throbbing near his abdomen.

By this point, the nightmarish sounds surrounded him, and he almost wished his hearing wasn't slowly coming back. The ship was groaning and shrieking as the floodwaters tore boilers loose from their fittings. Even though the equipment down there weighed thousands of tons, it was no match for the wall of ocean water that barraged it at whatever speed the ship was still moving.

He reached a door and found it closed. This door had a manual crank, so he reached down and tried to turn it. The effort was excruciating because of his injury, but he forced himself to use both arms, anyway. The wheel used to secure the door wouldn't budge. He strained even harder, but there was still no movement. By now the water was up to his thighs, and he knew it was a matter of minutes, maybe seconds, before it was too late. If he didn't get the door open, he would simply float up to the ceiling, where he would be trapped. Because he was at the extreme aft end of the section, it would be the last place to lose air, so he would float up there as the water slowly hemmed him in. Of course, the pressure of the air that remained would increase as the water flooded in—to the point that it would burst his eardrums, and then his eyes, and then his very skin would hemorrhage. He'd heard stories from his father about just that sort of thing. Hopefully he would pass out before too much of that happened. Regardless, the water would eventually fill the compartment, likely blowing out the bulkhead door that he was working on so frantically right now, and then it would pass into the next section until it eventually filled the whole ship.

Get control! he thought. *It does no good to imagine how you're going to die!* He needed to get control of himself if he wanted to live. *Okay, if I can't get this open, what next? Are there any escape hatches?* His mind raced to remember the various diagrams his mother had made him study when he was first assigned to the ship. It had made him angry that she insisted that he and Bill study all the safety diagrams that Cunard had sent home with them. They were probably the only two employees to even open the packets. But now he was frantically going over them in his mind. *There's a chance!* He remembered there was a ventilation shaft up at the top of this compartment, but to get to it he would have to wait for the compartment to fill with water, and then he'd swim to that spot. If he could get the grate off, there was a chance he could pull himself into the shaft and work his way to the next deck up.

Just as he was resigning himself to that slim hope, he felt something soft slam into his side. "What the . . ." He turned to see another man, much larger even than Avery, joining him at the crank. The fellow's face was cut and bleeding, and he didn't say a word. But together they twisted with all their might until suddenly the mechanism turned slightly.

"We're doing it!" Avery shouted joyously. "Keep turning!"

The man didn't even acknowledge him. He might not have even consciously recognized that Avery was there, but it didn't matter, because with their combined strength they were able to force the mechanism to open. Of course, there was enough water behind them now that it blew the door open, and they were sucked through along with a torrent of water.

"We should close the door!" Avery shouted, but the fellow simply shook his head. The volume of water flooding through was clearly too great for them to push against. So now they had compromised this compartment. "Let's go!" shouted Avery. "I know a way out!" He had forgotten for a while that he really did know the way. Having traveled this way with Bill just two days earlier, when he went up top to fix that plumbing, he realized there was an opening to one of the funnels close by. If they could get inside the funnel, they could climb up the steel ladder inside. Normally, it would be excruciatingly hot from the coal smoke, but with the boilers all going underwater, they might have a chance.

"Are you sure you know a way out?" the man asked, finally breaking his silence.

"I know a way. I'm not sure it will work, but we have limited options here."

As they started running in the direction of the escape hatch, they heard terrified shouting coming through the ventilation pipes overhead. Avery distinctly heard, "Let us out of here! We're in the elevator. It's stopped. Let us out!"

"The electricity! The elevators won't run. And with the ship listing this badly, the pulleys have likely fouled." Avery turned and looked at his unknown companion. "The men—they got on the elevators. Now they're stuck. They're all going to drown!" He felt as if he was going to vomit. He had to shake his head to clear the image of all those men trapped in the elevator cage as the water rose around them.

“They wouldn’t let me on the elevator . . . They said it was too full, that I was too big.” The man choked back his tears. Avery saw a look of hurt and anger in the fellow’s eyes, and it unnerved him.

“Come on!” Avery shouted. “We don’t have much time!”

* * *

“REVERSE ENGINES. FULL ASTERN!” Captain Turner watched in horror as the ship continued to surge ahead through the ocean. He had been standing on the starboard rail when the torpedo was spotted. Realizing that he was directly above the spot where it would strike, he’d hurried back onto the bridge.

Down in the engine room, the call for full astern was answered in an unfortunate way. As the forward turbines were disengaged, one of the assistant engineers brought the reverse turbines online before the propellers had stopped spinning. The thousands of finely tuned blades in the turbines were no match for the momentum of the turning propeller, and so they ground uselessly against each other. This caused the blades toward the rear of the turbine to spin backward while the steam flowing into the front of the turbine spinned the front blades in the correct direction. Thus, the turbines were forced to turn against themselves with a catastrophic increase in pressure building up against the incoming steam. The extremely high-pressure steam lines that fed the turbines burst under the pressure, and valves up and down the line ruptured, showering a blast of scalding steam on anyone who was in the area. With the loss of these lines, the pressure to the turbines dropped precipitously from 190 pounds per square inch to less than fifty. The *Lusitania* was completely out of control.

“Hard to port!” Turner hoped to bring the ship closer to shore to aid in a rescue, but he watched helplessly as his helmsman struggled to turn the wheel to no avail.

“We’ve lost power to the steering mechanism,” the helmsman said evenly. The man was a wonder, maintaining his calm while pandemonium reigned all around around him.

“I think it is safe to assume that the steam lines to the steering gear have ruptured,” said Staff Captain John Anderson. “We’ve lost electric power in many parts of the ship as well.” Anderson walked over to the trim indicator, which showed the ship listing some ten degrees to starboard. That meant they were taking on water far too rapidly for the bilge pumps to keep up. It also meant that the chances of isolating the flooding to a few compartments were unlikely. What they needed to do now was control the flooding.

Anderson continued by suggesting, "Perhaps we can counter the starboard list by flooding some of the port bulkheads," he added, "both to slow the ship and allow us to settle evenly in the water. At least we'd have more control over the flooding that way."

If Turner had heard him, he didn't acknowledge it. It was clear that the captain was in shock.

"We're listing . . ." Anderson went back to the indicator, ". . . eleven points to starboard. I don't see how we can stay afloat." He waited. "Captain—should we abandon ship?"

Turner looked about the cabin. The ship was skewing toward starboard, in spite of his order to turn to port. The skew was caused by the fearsome inrush of water where the torpedo had blown a hole in the side. Or was it two torpedoes? There had clearly been a second explosion. At any rate, the ship would eventually slow and stop, but it was going to sink very rapidly once it did. It was as if they were a long tube in the water now, with the hole that was open at the front scooping in ocean water by the thousands of tons as they moved forward. The sound of machinery tearing loose below was evidence of the incredible pressure accumulating in the bowels of the ship.

"Gentlemen. Abandon ship!" Captain Turner set in motion the procedures that would see the lifeboats swung out, the passengers loaded, and the ship abandoned. How much time did they have from the moment the torpedo struck until the *Lusitania* disappeared beneath the waves? Would there be enough time to complete an evacuation? Even now they knew that hundreds of people would die. Indeed, surely hundreds already had from the initial blast and flooding.

* * *

"THIS IS UNBELIEVABLE," SAID SCHWEIGER. "Take a look." He yielded the periscope to Lanz. "It appears as if the ship is sinking . . . But how is that possible with only one torpedo?"

Lanz stepped up to the periscope. "It's the *Lusitania*!" He backed away from the periscope in shock. "And we gave no warning! It makes no sense that it would go down so quickly with just one torpedo."

"I saw a second explosion," Schweiger explained. "Perhaps ammunition?" It would be marvelous if it was ammunition, because that would prove that the ship was carrying contraband and was therefore a legitimate military target.

"Or coal dust. This particular ship has coal bunkers between the outer and inner hull." Lanz was indeed an authority on English ships.

Schweiger nodded. "Whatever the reason, it appears that it will sink much faster than we could have ever expected." He turned to the men assembled on the bridge. "Why don't you each take a look." He then took turns with them, allowing a man to look, after which Schweiger would step forward and do a scan of the sea to see if any warships were approaching.

"Should we fire a second torpedo, just to be sure?" asked the torpedo officer.

"I don't see that it would accomplish anything. Impossible as it seems, I believe the ship will go down in less than half an hour with our first torpedo. There's no reason to waste a good torpedo when the damage is already sufficient."

Lanz happened to glance down to where Voegele was seated, his hands tied behind him. He would be a prisoner until they returned to port, where he would very likely be court-martialed. Glancing back through the periscope, Lanz could understand the man's reluctance, particularly now that hundreds of passengers were jumping, falling, or being pushed into the icy Atlantic. No one had ever sunk a passenger liner before, particularly without giving warning. Of course, the conundrum was that had they risen to give warning, the great ship would have poured on steam and escaped. Still, as he saw the hundreds of people flailing in the water, he admitted that it was a sight to sicken any man. Yet it was also a great victory for Germany. "Now we'll see what the world has to say."

* * *

BILL SHAFER WAS WORKING IN the first-class dining room when there was an odd thump that seemed to shake the ship—not so severe that any dishes were knocked off the tables, but enough that some of the passengers gasped in alarm. It felt as if they'd hit something, but of course that made no sense.

"What is it?" inquired one of the ladies.

"I'm not sure, ma'am. I'll try to find out." As Bill started to walk back to his serving station, he noticed that a number of guests—particularly the men—had abandoned their lunch to go outside and have a look for themselves. He wished he could join them.

It was just a matter of moments before someone came running back inside, shouting, "It's a torpedo! We've been hit by a torpedo!" That's when they felt a much more forceful second thump that did knock the plates around. This explosion and the man's announcement were accompanied by screams of alarm as nearly everyone jumped up from their seats, many knocking their chairs over. "It's a second torpedo!" someone shouted, although it was impossible to know just what was going on.

Unlike the passengers outside who had been dazed by witnessing the impact and explosion, the people inside the ship were in full command of their senses and were terrified by the news.

"I can feel us slowing down," someone shouted. "We should go faster to outrun the submarine." Bill shook his head at the absurdity of that statement; how do you outrun anything when you've got a hole in your side?

The chief steward said forcefully, "I need everyone to be calm! Please be calm. We have procedures for an event such as this, and the captain will tell us how to proceed." He'd have been just as successful telling people to remain calm if an asteroid had struck as in attempting to quiet the nerves of the people in the dining saloon at this moment. Passengers were running for the doors—probably not knowing where they were going, but running nonetheless.

"Excuse me. Waiter!" Bill turned to see an elegantly dressed matron waving to him.

"Yes, ma'am." It was hard for him to remain calm, because he couldn't help but wonder what had happened to Avery down belowdecks. He was below the waterline, after all.

"I know this is an inconvenient time, but perhaps you could warm our coffee," she said with an amiable, unhurried smile.

"I'd be glad to, of course. But perhaps you should go directly to your cabin to get your life jackets on. Just in case the captain wants people to take to the lifeboats." He tried to say this as evenly as possible, which was hard given the urgency he felt.

The elderly gentleman seated next to her smiled and said, "We won't be doing that. Whatever fate has in store for us, we will face it together. But this isn't the time to get excited."

"Yes, sir." Bill raced to his station, grabbed the sterling silver server, and made a dash back to the table.

"Here you go." He poured the coffee and then set the server on another table so it wouldn't spill on them. "My brother. He works down below. I really should . . ." Bill stopped, torn between his duty and the urgency to find his brother.

A look of recognition dawned on the couple. "Oh, dear," said the woman. "We mustn't keep you. You go. We'll be fine."

"Are you sure? I'd be glad to take you to your cabin. You really should . . ."

They waved him away and sat placidly drinking their coffee as if it were a delightful Sunday afternoon in a sidewalk café. But Bill couldn't wait. Dashing out the door, he went out onto the deck. *I've got to get to Avery.* By this point after the torpedo strike, he saw some grimy men emerging from belowdecks, their faces scalded and bleeding, bodies covered in coal dust turned to mud from head to foot.

"Oh, Avery!" Bill didn't know what to do. It would be impossible to find his brother below. Besides, if he were still alive, he'd make it out his own way and would probably pass Bill if he tried to go down.

Realizing he could do nothing for Avery, his thoughts raced on.

"Mr. Stringham! I've got to help Mr. Stringham." He took off at a dead run toward the first-class cabins.

But as he neared the porthole door, an officer shouted to him, "You there! Steward. Come help us. The captain has given the order to abandon ship, and we need to control the crowd. People are trying to leap into the lifeboats, even though they're still fifty feet above the water. We've got to control the crowd until we can lower the boats in an orderly fashion."

"But I've got to help my passengers . . ."

"Someone else will help them. We need you now! That's an order."

Bill felt desperate, but there was nothing to do but obey. Everyone's life mattered equally, and he had to do his best to help those closest at hand. As he raced to the railing, he was sickened to see how far the ship was listing to starboard. Even now people were sliding toward the rails as they tried to make their way forward to wherever they thought an open boat was. He also noticed that the canvas boats, which were supposed to provide excess capacity beyond the lifeboats, were being trampled on as people headed for the wooden lifeboats dangling from their davits. He could only imagine that the canvas would be torn to shreds, ruining the boats before they even left the deck.

"Dear Lord, please help us!" He ran to grab one of the lines that held a swaying lifeboat. Some people had already jumped into the lifeboat, making it very difficult for the ship's crew who were holding it in place. He added his muscles to the task, but with the crush of passengers, it felt as if it would be hopeless.

* * *

"I CAN'T GO ON."

Avery turned to his companion. The big fellow hadn't uttered a single complaint as they crawled their way through the tangles of wires and mountains of debris. The route Avery had chosen seemed abandoned by everyone else, and it was as if the two of them were all alone on the great ship—two warriors left alone to pit their lives against the dying ship.

"But you must. We're almost there—I promise."

"I'm . . . I'm wounded."

Avery turned back and crawled to where his friend had collapsed on the floor. By this point they had escaped the onrushing water, at least for a few minutes. There was even daylight streaming in from the open door that would lead them inside the funnel. It was a dangerous thing to undertake, but he didn't know any other way out.

"Where? Where are you hurt?"

The fellow pulled back his shirt to show a ghastly wound in his stomach. In this light, which perhaps allowed Avery to see the man for the first time, Avery saw his trousers were soaked in blood. The sight was revolting, and he wanted to rush to the doorway and freedom, but instead he sat down next to him. In spite of the urgency, it seemed the right thing to do, and, as an added benefit, sitting down took some pressure from his own wound.

"How did it happen?"

"The handle of my shovel. When the torpedo hit us, I was thrown off balance and fell right onto my shovel. The wood snapped from my weight, and the jagged end stabbed me."

"How did you make it this far?"

The man shrugged. "Adrenaline, I guess. Fear lets you do things you wouldn't think possible." He sagged. "But it's all gone now."

"You'll be fine. We're going to rest for one full minute, and then we'll crawl our way to that door. Once we get there, you'll go first, and I'll push you from below."

"That would be great." The man's breathing was labored now.

"What's your name?"

"Julian Edwards."

"Mine is Avery Shafer."

The man's chest heaved violently as he struggled for air. His hand tightened on Avery's. "Thank you, Shafer."

"For what? You saved my life. I couldn't get that door open by myself."

"For staying with me."

Avery felt his throat tighten. He knew they were out of time, but he didn't want to leave this man alone. No one should die alone. "Hold on. For just another minute . . ."

But it was too late. Edwards's head slumped against Avery as he took a final gasp.

"Oh, my." Avery tried gently shaking Edwards but to no avail. Then he tried to find a pulse without success.

"I've never seen anyone die!" said Avery to the darkness. "This can't be happening." He gulped a few times, trying to control the pain in his throat. "You've got to get going. There's nothing to be done for him now . . ." Wise as that thought was, he found himself wanting to just sit there. "Perhaps Edwards is the lucky one." And at that moment, it did feel safe there. Even the noise from the other parts of the ship seemed dampened. "I'll just sit and catch my breath."

Then the bulkhead door exploded. They'd passed through it perhaps two minutes earlier when the water was just up to their ankles.

Now the previous compartment must have filled completely—a sign of how fast the ship was sinking. With the pressure of countless tons of seawater pressing against it, the door didn't stand a chance. The ocean was making it clear that it had no intention of being held back by mere steel. When the door gave way, a blast of water shot into the compartment where Avery was sitting with roughly the force of a fire hydrant opened to full blast, except with perhaps ten to twenty times the volume. Even though it was just the edge of the stream that hit him, it nearly knocked him senseless. Had the full force hit him, he'd have been killed on the spot. He scrambled to the doorway that led into the great funnel and then swung himself inside, his feet desperately searching for a foothold.

"There it is!" He grabbed for a rung of the ladder and planted his feet as firmly as possible on one of the rungs. The list of the ship was so great now that the weight of his body pulled him onto the ladder. The list actually made it easier to start climbing. It also meant that the residual smoke and heat was concentrated at what was now the top side of the funnel, above and away from him. Even so, it was still very much like being in an extremely hot sauna, and the fumes caused him to choke.

"You've got a long way to climb," he said to himself. "But nothing that you can't do." To make it from the lowest decks of the ship to the top of the funnel was going to be a challenge, but adrenaline was definitely still working for him.

"What the—!" said Avery in alarm. A great gust of air and smoke almost blew him off the ladder. Regaining his handhold, he started climbing again. As the water had forced its way farther into the ship, it had displaced the air, and the funnel offered the perfect route for the air to escape.

Avery's stomach muscles tightened as a new realization dawned on him—a new danger building up gradually below him.

Chapter 18
In the Water

"Come on, Stringham . . . Wake up!"

Everett Stringham was aggravated that something was interrupting his walk through the park in Evanston. Annie was by his side, and the late afternoon sun was setting the sky ablaze in the glorious colors of sunset. It was about his favorite way to end a day.

"Stringham! Wake up!" The slap on his face that followed brought him to consciousness with a start.

"What? What is it?" His thoughts raced wildly as he tried to sort out where he was. His arm hurt him terribly.

"Good. You're awake. We've got to get your life jacket on and get moving."

Everett rubbed his eyes with his good hand. "John Todd? Is that you?"

Todd nodded and started to lift Everett to his feet. "There's no time. The ship is going down too fast."

A new wave of panic swept over Everett as he finally remembered his predicament. The ship had been torpedoed, and he'd been making his way to his cabin to get a life jacket.

"Yes, of course! My life jacket—it's right over there." John Todd had already found the life jacket and was making his way quickly toward Everett.

"Here—lift your arms, and I'll tie the jacket on." Everett winced as he lifted his injured arm, but Todd was careful so as to cause the least amount of pain.

"Don't pass out on me, Stringham. I'm not strong enough to drag you—we've got too many passageways to maneuver our way through."

Everett was breathing rapidly, but he concentrated.

"There. You've got it. You'll be one of the few to have it tied on right. The people who designed these things didn't consider how hard they'd be to use, particularly in an emergency."

"Do we go forward or aft?" Everett asked.

"I want to say forward, but the bow is already underwater. We may find the ocean before we find an escape. I think we need to go aft."

That was easier said than done, considering the tilt of the ship. No longer were they walking down a level corridor but rather making their way up a steep incline with no railings to hold on to.

"You get in front of me, and I'll push you if needs be," Todd offered.

"Thank you. I appreciate it."

"Don't waste time talking, just move!"

Everett moved. As fast as his legs and lungs would take him. He only turned around once—just long enough to see that the water had already reached the door to his cabin. "I can't believe it's happening this fast!" he said breathlessly.

"Just move! We've got to get out to the deck. Otherwise we'll drown in here." Amazing as it seemed, it was proving almost impossible to outrun the advancing water. It wasn't really the water that was advancing but the ship that was sinking beneath them. "Run!"

Everett strained as hard as he could, particularly when one of the doors to the deck came into view.

"That's it, Stringham. You can make it!" Everett was gasping for air, but at least he didn't feel any pain in his arm. With a mighty heave, he reached the door and turned his back to it while using his good hand to open the knob.

"Here we go, then," shouted Todd, who had come up to his side and now pushed with him on the door. As the door fell open toward the sea, they both fell out onto the deck, landing in a tumble against a portion of the wall that jutted out toward the railing. It was fortunate the jut was there—otherwise they would have found themselves sliding down the deck and into the water.

"Not as hard to open as we thought it would be, was it?" Todd said.

"*You* have a sense of humor, John? Who would have ever thought that of you?"

"Promise not to tell anyone. It would completely ruin my reputation with the crew."

The two of them lay in a heap on the deck, gasping for breath. In spite of the pandemonium around them—people screaming as they fell forward toward the water . . . lifeboats crashing against the sinking ship—they had no more energy for the moment.

"Thank you for coming for me." Everett inhaled deeply. "I'm sure you saved my life." When Todd failed to respond, he added, "What do we next?"

"We go into the water. It's too late for a lifeboat. They've either been launched by this point or have crashed into the ocean."

"Crashed?"

Todd nodded. "People were jumping into the boats like a bunch of fools. The crew members holding the ropes couldn't hold the weight, and many a boat tipped into the ocean, spilling people from high above the water. Then the boat would come crashing down on top of them. It's the most horrible thing I've ever seen."

Everett nodded. "To the water, then."

"You'll have to do your best to swim, Stringham. The problem we have is that with the ship tipped this far forward, it's going to create a huge suction as more of it starts to go under. We've got to get away, if we can. Otherwise we'll be pulled under and drown."

Everett winced at the image. "All right. It's now or never." Everett moved gingerly out further on the deck, just as a body came sliding past him, crashing with a sickening crunch against the very wall they'd been huddled against.

"Just let go," said Todd. "We have a clear path to the water."

With a shout, Everett Stringham let himself go as he started a slide into the frigidly cold water of the Irish Sea.

* * *

"ALMOST THERE . . ."

"You can make it. But you've got to hurry! The funnel will collapse at any moment!"

It turned out that Avery wasn't the only one to think of the funnel. In fact, there were a number of coal-stained men working their way to the top. The fellow who was encouraging him was at the top of the funnel. Those who were still in the funnel could almost walk horizontally, so great was the tilt to the ship. In what Americans would call a bear crawl, Avery used both his hands and legs to scurry toward the imposing maw of the funnel, where he'd have another problem to figure out—how to get down to the deck, since the funnel was now suspended almost horizontally above the deck and water. The ladder on the outside would leave them dangling uselessly in the air if they tried to use it. *You can figure that out when you get there.*

"Hurry!"

As if to punctuate the warning, there was a groaning sound that might have been a warning that the metal of the funnel was starting to buckle. Avery moved faster.

He was so absorbed in reaching his goal that the sound that started to echo below and behind him didn't register. First, there was the sound of wrenching metal, which by now had become common. But this time proved different. Second, there was the sound of a small explosion, perhaps a major bulkhead giving way, perhaps destroyed by a furnace or boiler crashing down on it. At any rate, the third thing that happened caused a terrible roar like the sound of a giant foghorn and then a blast of air and soot that knocked the air out of his lungs. So violent was the blast that Avery couldn't fully appreciate its force until it launched him up and out of the funnel, blowing him and the chap who had been cheering him along in a great arc out and above the water. It was such a surreal scene that he struggled to grasp what was happening, even though he was suddenly chilled as his body sailed out the funnel and into the open air, no longer heated by the exhaust gases inside the funnel. Both he and the other fellow screamed when they were able to gasp some air. In perhaps the most unreal part of the experience, he saw hundreds of floundering bodies in the water below him. He tried to calculate the point where he would hit the water. Without a life jacket, and nothing to protect him from the impact, he thought quickly of what to do and then forced all the air out of his lungs, curled his body up into a ball, and closed his eyes.

* * *

"MR. STRINGHAM! MR. TODD!"

"Sit down, you fool!"

Bill reluctantly sat down in the lifeboat but turned to the officer in charge and said desperately, "But it's Mr. Stringham and Mr. Todd. They're going in the water. We've got to go to them. It's my supervisor and . . . my friend!"

"I don't care if it's Winston Churchill," the officer replied, disdain thick in his voice. "We're not going near that ship. Do you see how fast it's going down? It would suck us under for sure!" The murmur from the passengers in the boat assured Bill that they'd throw him overboard if he tried.

"But they'll never make it if we don't go back . . ."

One of the ladies whose cabin he had cared for, Mrs. Ruth Jones, reached out and touched his hand. "Perhaps they'll be all right." They both knew the odds were against that, but what else was there to say? Bill fought back tears.

"Isn't it awful," someone said. Bill turned and followed their gaze. The sight that confronted them was truly awful. The stern of the mighty *Lusitania* was even now lifting up and out of the water, the great propellers still turning.

"Look, someone's hanging by a rope above that propeller," one of the survivors called out.

In their shocked state, that was a horrible thing to consider. Some cheered when the man managed to pull himself back up and onto the deck, only to start sliding at breakneck speed along the length of the deck toward the water.

"I can't look," said Mrs. Jones.

"It's a miracle that we got our ship steady in the water. Just look at all the others." Without any lifeboat drills, virtually no one knew the correct way to board a lifeboat, which is why so many boats ended up crashing uselessly into the sea. Only a handful landed right side up. Some of the boats had turned over in the water, and desperate people were trying to pull themselves up on top of the slippery hulls. In other places the canvas boats were swamped, filled with water but still floating. They at least provided a place for people to sit, even though their lower bodies were covered in icy water. Mostly, there were just bodies in the water—some with life jackets, many without. And there was blood. The blue waters of the ocean had turned crimson, particularly near bodies that were floating facedown in the water.

"What's that?" asked the officer of the small craft, Lieutenant Ames. "The ship just shuddered and stopped!"

Everyone turned to look and were amazed by the phenomenon.

"It's just sitting there . . ."

Lieutenant Ames realized what was happening. "The bow has hit the bottom. The ship is longer than the sea is deep, and the bow has planted itself right in the bottom of the ocean floor."

"Is that possible?" someone asked.

"You're seeing it with your own eyes! It must be possible."

"We were that close to shore? How is that possible?" asked by a gentleman who had already demonstrated his knowledge of nautical affairs—a weekend sailor from Massachusetts.

Lieutenant Ames simply shook his head. "Any place would have been better than where we are—but we didn't know that at the time. Now I think we'll all be grateful that we're so close to shore."

"Look—it's starting to settle," a survivor said.

In a scene that even the craziest nightmare could not have envisioned, the giant ship slowly started to fall backward on itself. With the bow anchored in the ocean bottom, the weight of the ship started its final dance with death.

For some lucky souls who were still clinging to the superstructure, it offered one last chance to get away as the falling ship brought them closer to the water. For others, it would bring their efforts to escape to an ignominious end as they were sucked under by the vacuum that would be created as the hull went under the water.

In just a matter of moments, the funnels started collapsing into the ocean, crushing anyone in the water where they struck. Boilers exploded, sending great waterspouts of steam and water into the air. The sound of furnaces and equipment breaking loose inside the ship rumbled out across the ears of the frightened survivors. Finally, the great propellers splashed back into the water for the last time. All was accompanied by an increasing crescendo of noise and mayhem as the ship broke apart in an agony of wrenching steel and human wails. It was a scene that would haunt survivors for the rest of their lives.

The drama took a personal turn in Bill's lifeboat.

"Help me!" Everyone in the boat turned to see a forlorn creature calling and waving his arms from some wreckage he was holding on to.

"Make for that man," said the officer.

"No!" someone shouted. "There's no room! We'll sink if we bring any other people on."

"We've got to help him," said Bill.

The crowd grew very ugly, very quickly. "Not and drown ourselves," said a man toward the back of the boat.

"But we have to," Bill declared firmly. "It could just as easily be one of us out there."

"But it's not. We're here, and we want to stay alive!"

The general disagreement escalated, with roughly half the passengers urging them to row away from the man and the other half urging them to row toward him.

"I'm in charge here, and you'll do what I say!" declared Lieutenant Ames. To emphasize the point, he reached down to his side and unstrapped a handgun he held on his hip. "And I said row! Now those of you with oars, start rowing toward the man." When one fellow on an oar still hesitated, the officer pointed his gun directly at him. "If you don't obey me, we'll make room for the other fellow in short order!"

Bill was electrified by this development and wanted to let out a cheer. Some did, while others who had urged them to row away simply slunk down in their seats as if to disappear. But they all got the message, and the man on the oar started rowing with the others. In a matter of minutes they had the fellow in the water within their grasp, and some of the men reached out and pulled him into the boat. As soon as they dragged him out of the water, a wound on his face started bleeding.

"Here," said an elderly passenger. "Use this." She handed Bill a fine linen handkerchief, which he used to apply pressure to the wound.

"Now, let's start working our way toward shore," said the officer. "We are indeed full, or I'd order us to go back for other survivors. But if we come across anyone else, we *will* make space for them. Is that understood?"

This order was confirmed by a general murmur.

"Fine. We'll take turns on the oars. We don't have to go fast, since rescue boats will be coming out to meet us. But I want to shorten the distance as much as possible just in case . . ."

"Just in case what?" asked one of the men.

"Nothing. I just want to get closer to shore. It's only logical."

"Just in case *what*? You were going to say something."

"Just in case that submarine decides to take another shot at us," the fellow from Massachusetts replied.

"They wouldn't do that," said Ruth Jones.

"They just sunk an unarmed passenger liner with more than two thousand people on board. What makes you think they'd hesitate to shoot us with their deck gun now?"

"Eliminate all the witnesses," someone else said.

"That will be enough of that," Ames snapped. "You men on the oars just row. The rest of you, save your strength. Talking does no good now, and it's going to get cold soon enough."

* * *

"IT'S GONE!" SCHWEIGER COULD NOT fully conceal his astonishment.

"Eighteen minutes," said Lanz. "Just eighteen minutes to kill the greatest ship in the oceans."

"Well, this will prove a historic day!" Schweiger turned to the crew. "Congratulations, gentlemen. You just struck a mighty blow against England—perhaps a decisive blow."

The crew let out a cheer.

"Rescue boats will be coming—perhaps some British warships," someone offered.

Schweiger bit his lip as he considered this. The chance to shoot another ship, or even two, was tempting. But it was one thing to sink a passenger liner—there was no longer any question about it possibly being a troopship—and quite another to go after the rescue boats. The international press would make a great deal out of that. Not to mention that the English would be out for revenge, and he didn't relish the thought of enduring a pitched battle against enemy destroyers.

"We will head out to sea and watch what happens. For now it makes no sense to add to this accomplishment." Not one to second-guess his own orders, Schweiger gave directions and then excused himself to his cabin.

Lanz was thoughtful. As the ship purred through the water on its electric motors, he reached for a piece of paper and a slide rule.

Calculating the distance from where they fired, the speed of their boat, and the speed of the *Lusitania,* he wrote some figures on the paper. He shook his head. "Five seconds earlier or twenty seconds later, and we would have missed. A window of twenty-five seconds was all we had." He glanced over at Voegele and whispered to himself, "What would have happened had you passed the order on instantly, my young idealist? Would the torpedo have passed in front of the ship?"

Lanz bit his lip. Was it possible that Voegele's humanity and compassion were in part responsible for this great calamity? How ironic. He thought about going and telling the young man. But to what end? He was miserable enough as it stood. Lanz tore up the piece of paper and made his way to the galley for a meal.

* * *

"Take it, Stringham!"

"I can't—you're hurt even worse than me. You climb on."

Todd shook his head. "Please." He hesitated before adding, "I want you to do it."

Reluctantly, Everett allowed himself to be thrust onto a large piece of debris, some kind of wooden patio table that had come up from the depths of the ocean with Everett and Todd. In fact, it was this table that had struck a potentially mortal blow to John Todd.

"There. I'm on. Certainly you can hang on as well?" Everett asked.

"I'll try." Todd's face was pale, and Everett could only guess at the pain he was in.

As the great ship went down, Todd had yelled at Everett to hold his breath and start pulling to the surface with everything he had. As predicted, they were both sucked under the surface of the water by the vacuum created by the sinking ship. Everett had plunged down until he thought his lungs and eardrums would burst. He tried as hard as he could to swim up to the surface, but the *Lusitania*'s pull just kept dragging him farther. He knew that in a matter of moments, he would be forced to take an involuntary gasp for air, but just then he felt something on his neck and turned to see John Todd pulling with him. With Todd's help, Everett worked even harder, and miraculously they managed to pull free of the suction. In what seemed an eternity, they rose toward the light and broke free to the surface. He had separated from Todd as their ascent had accelerated. After taking in great gulps of air, he turned to see that John Todd had made it too. Just as Everett was waving at him, this table had come bursting up from the depths, smashing into John Todd from below. Everett had recoiled in horror as he saw Todd's body thrown up and out of the water. The table settled in the water, and Todd was thrashing about in agony when Everett reached him. He was quite sure that both of John Todd's legs had been broken. From the stain in the water, one might even have been amputated or at least severely wounded. Now Todd was calm, which seemed even more ominous.

"Let me pull you on."

"We'd both sink—you stay put."

Everett lay back on the table. He was struggling as he learned to keep his balance on the thing, but at least he was mostly out of the water and supported. That would make the ordeal of waiting for the rescue boats an easier task.

"John . . ." He looked into Todd's eyes. The pain must have been terrible, because Todd could only blink in response. "You saved my life. Thank you."

Todd took a deep breath and forced himself to speak. "Listen, Stringham—Everett—I'm sorry about that night. I was drunk . . ."

"It's all right . . ."

"No! It's not. That's not who I am. I'm sorry."

"You're forgiven. I promise that you are forgiven."

"My sister . . ." Todd's voice faded, and Everett leaned far out into the water so he could hear what John Todd was whispering.

* * *

AVERY SHAFER GASPED FOR AIR while coughing up seawater. For a moment, he thought he saw blood in what he had coughed up—which would be understandable given the force with which he hit the water. His side was now a dull ache, but unbelievable as it seemed, he had survived his trip through the air—as had a couple of others.

Avery regained consciousness just in time to turn and witness the last great gasp of the *Lusitania* as it slipped beneath the waves. He watched with a sense of fascinated horror as the funnel he had escaped through broke loose from the superstructure and came crashing down into the water. Had he been just two or three minutes later in making it to the top of the funnel, he would have been in it as it collapsed.

Once again, it's you who saved me, Mum. Bill and I hated those swimming lessons when we were young, but now they're keeping me alive. He thought this while treading the water with his hands and feet. As mere boys, Avery and Bill had gone down to the creek with their mother, where more experienced boys liked to skinny dip, and she paid a small sum to the best of them to teach her boys how to swim. Now Avery found himself in the midst of a great crowd of people splashing furiously in the water as they struggled to stay alive, while he more easily kept his hands moving beneath the surface.

Avery started swimming through the water in search of a piece of debris. There was plenty to be had, although most of the really serviceable pieces had already been taken by those who were not unconscious after they hit the water. At last he spied a broken deck chair and started swimming to it. As he neared it, he saw that he was in competition with some other swimmer just a bit further off. Avery swam as fast as he could and reached the chair before the young woman. She looked at him with a look of contempt and fear, and with just a moment's hesitation he pushed the chair in her direction. He was pleased by the shock this caused her. Then he swam backward before he had to talk to her about it.

After perhaps half an hour in the frigid water, he felt himself slowing down, and his body felt heavy in the water. It was only then that he realized he'd been swimming all this time with his shoes on. *That alone could kill you, you idiot.* So he reached down in the water and pried his shoes off, allowing them to sink to the bottom of the ocean. Although his feet were colder, he also felt it easier to stay afloat. He stripped off his shirt and his trousers, leaving only his underwear.

As if fate felt indebted to him for his act of chivalry to the young woman, he was surprised to bump his head against a great wooden chest. Turning around, he was pleased to find that no one else had claimed it. The thing was huge—large enough, in fact, that Avery could pull himself on top of it with a fair degree of stability. His side ache made it difficult to pull himself up, but through sheer force of will and some very well-developed muscles, he made it. Once on top, he wished he had his clothes back. Still, he was out of the water, and in a few minutes the breeze had dried his skin. *Maybe I have a chance, after all.*

* * *

THERE WERE PEOPLE IN QUEENSTOWN, Ireland, who actually saw the explosion from shore. At ten miles out, the *Lusitania* was tall enough that she was visible with the naked eye. Coast watchers up on the hillsides with glasses could see it all with even more clarity, and they immediately raised the alarm.

But faster than any visual sighting was the SOS signal that the radio operator of the *Lusitania* had started broadcasting almost the moment the torpedo struck. Bob Leith was an incredibly brave man who stayed at his wireless station pounding out the SOS emergency distress message, "Come at once, big list off south Head, Old Kinsale," over and over again on his Morse code key. He stayed at it right up to the moment the water was about to flood the bridge. He may have been the next-to-last person off the ship. The honor of being last was claimed by Captain Turner, who waited until the bridge itself was awash and the stern was settling before he mounted one of the lookout towers to wait for the water to come up around him.

Of course, hundreds never made it off the ship, trapped as they were belowdecks while the water flooded in upon them. Turner would have drowned at sea had it not been for the simple act of the sun gleaming momentarily off one of the golden buttons on his jacket—creating a flicker on the horizon that a sharp-eyed passenger in one of the lifeboats saw. When they found Turner, he was unconscious and nearly dead from hypothermia. Some of the passengers wanted to kill him on the spot, but humanity prevailed in the end.

At the Admiralty in London, the admirals who had been so guarded and vague in their communications to the *Lusitania* about the deadly peril they were sailing into were stunned to learn that she had sunk. All had believed it impossible. Perhaps that's why it was never communicated to Captain Turner that the *U-20* had already sunk three ships in the area before the *Lusy* arrived—which meant he sailed with less urgency than he might have if he had been informed by the Admiralty.

The Admiralty also didn't explain satisfactorily why they hadn't sent an escort to help her through the troubled waters. The excuse given for that was that there weren't enough warships to go around and that it was not the duty of the navy to shepherd each and every merchant ship on the ocean. Most people thought the *Lusitania* was hardly a normal merchant ship and were furious that she'd been left on her own. Now the Admiralty had to move quickly to transfer any blame from their Lordships to Captain Turner and the Cunard Line. To admit error on their part would be to shake the nation's confidence in the judgment of its leaders—a potentially fatal injury to morale in a time of war.

Fortunately, the people of Queenstown were animated not by political concerns but by the urgent desire to help those in need in the waters so near their home. And so a small armada of tiny surface ships immediately set out into the ocean. Some were rowboats, others small fishing trawlers with sails, and a few with small steam engines. None of them were fast, and it was three o'clock in the afternoon. It would be almost dark before they could reach the survivors.

Chapter 19

Rescue Ships in Sight

"Over there—there's a woman and a baby." Bill felt the despair of the people in the boat when they heard this, but no one resisted when the men on the oars made off for her. After two hours in the open air, people were shivering, some uncontrollably, in what was the clearest evidence yet that they were freezing to death.

"Here you go, ma'am," someone called out encouragingly as the distance narrowed. Strong hands lifted her out of the water, still holding the baby in her arms. As people shifted in their seats to accommodate her, Mrs. Jones looked down kindly at the baby, only to have her breath catch as she stifled a sob. After all that the poor thing had been through, the baby had closed its eyes forever.

"I'm so sorry," said Ruth Jones.

The woman looked at her child for a few moments and then said in a tearful voice, "Let me bury my baby." With a simple dignity that survived in spite of her exhaustion, she set the lifeless infant in the water, where it floated peacefully on the sea.

Every now and then someone would try to strike up a tune, and while no one objected to hearing that person sing or whistle, very few joined in. As the waves slapped into the side of the little boat, sprays of salt water would sometimes splash into the faces of those closest to the sides. At first they tried to shelter themselves by raising an arm or garment, but eventually they resigned themselves to the discomfort. With time, nearly everyone in the boat looked like they were covered in ice, even though it was just caked salt that had hardened on their skin and clothes.

"There! I see a ship! It's coming to us."

That roused the whole boat.

"Raise your oars above your heads," ordered Lieutenant Ames.

The men whose turn it was to row quickly complied, while the others started cheering. "They've got to be big—just look at all the smoke they're making."

"Steaming for us at full speed," said another passenger happily.

"It will be just like the other two that we spotted," another said. "They both turned away."

"Why did they do that?" asked Mrs. Jones. "Surely they had to know we are here. Why would they come so close, only to leave us?" She looked out into the water. "We still have a chance, but so many of those in the water have already died. Why would they leave them?"

"Torpedoes is my guess," said Bill. "I recognized those ships, the *City of Exeter* and the *Etonian*. They wouldn't have broken off unless they were worried for their own safety."

"And how do you know that?" asked Lieutenant Ames.

Bill turned to the back of the boat. "I live in Liverpool. Friends of my father work on those ships. They've been working with Standard Oil in the United States to transfer oil into the port." He stopped talking, realizing that it didn't really matter who the ships belonged to; the fact was that they had come within a close distance of the wreckage, only to break off at the last moment.

"Do you really think the Germans are still around?" asked the fellow from Massachusetts. "They have to be worried about the Royal Navy coming after them."

"You would think so," said one of the more belligerent passengers. "Not only did the King's navy fail to escort us, but they're nowhere to be seen now that our ship's on the bottom of the ocean and we're freezing to death out here!"

Bill expected Lieutenant Ames to tell them to be quiet, but Ames simply stared at his shoes. He probably agreed with the man.

"Like I said earlier, they want to get rid of the evidence."

Some people actually murmured their assent. Gruesome as it sounded, having first been applied to the Germans who had torpedoed them, it struck a raw nerve to think that the British Admiralty was ignoring them now—particularly after all the assurances Captain Turner had given them.

"Well, none of that matters now," said Mrs. Jones. "Because that ship right there is going to save us!"

"And your belief is going to make it true?" asked a particularly negative survivor.

It was not surprising to Bill that the skeptics never told anyone their names.

"I don't need to believe it. I can see with my own eyes . . ."

"Really?" said the fellow smugly. "Then tell me why that ship has now turned away."

People had been so engaged in the dialog that they had looked away from their rescuers for a moment. Now they all whirled in that direction, including Bill.

"No!" another lady shouted. "Come back!" She stood up and started shouting hysterically, "Come back! You've got to come back!" But it didn't come back. Whether frightened by a submarine or through sheer indifference, it was clearly sailing west on a perpendicular course that would never intersect their location.

"We're lost," said one of the women.

"If there are German submarines in the area, I wish they'd surface and shoot us! Better to die quickly than freeze to death out here with the shore in sight."

"That'll be enough of that!" said Lieutenant Ames. "There's been no sub activity in the last two hours, and there's not likely to be. It's one thing for a warship to sail out to us—that is a perfect invitation for any Germans that may be lurking about. But you can all see the smaller craft coming out, so I want no more talk that suggests anything other than a rescue."

* * *

As bad as it was for the survivors in the lifeboat, it was far worse for those in the water—or in their underwear on a steamer trunk.

"Maybe a few more minutes?" he pleaded with himself. The strategy he was about to employ was risky, but he didn't know what else to do. "If only you'd thought of it first!" He was aggravated with himself for having failed to think of it before he had dried off.

The advice he'd given himself was that he needed to crawl off the chest into the water where he could open it and hopefully find some dry clothes or linens or something else that he could wrap himself in. Of course the problem with that was that he'd get wet again, and he wasn't sure that there would be anything made of fabric inside, so it might just make things worse. Even if he was successful, he didn't know if he'd have the strength to pull himself back up on the chest. "You would have had the energy if you'd have done it an hour ago!" Of course he hadn't done it an hour ago, because it had seemed reasonable that rescuers would be arriving at any time, so why go through the shock of getting back into the water? But to everyone in the area's dismay, the rescuers hadn't come, and here they were still stuck in the ice water as the sun dropped in the western sky. *You'll die for sure if the sun goes down and you're fully exposed like this.* He thought about it for a moment. *You'll die anyway if you're out here all night.* Laughing, he slipped into the water, which took his breath right away. It was difficult to fumble with the locks of the steamer, particularly with his hands all closed from the salt and cold.

He was so intent on what he was doing that he almost missed seeing the fellow swimming toward him.

"Stop!" he tried to shout, although his voice was puny and pathetic. Clearing his throat, he tried again. "Stop! This is my trunk! You leave me alone!"

"You got off it! It's fair game!" the fellow called back. Avery peered through salt-tortured eyes to try to take the measure of his adversary. He was mostly covered in water, but his head and face made it look like he was pretty burly.

Shouting to the man in the water, he said, "You'll have to take it away from me, and I've spent the last year throwing coal in the boilers of the *Lusitania*! So I'll throw you right into eternity if you keep coming!" It was hard to believe that he was acting like this, but it was now life and death. He watched as the fellow kept coming, and he actually pulled himself up as high out of the water as he could so the idiot could see his torso.

The fellow stopped and hit the water, sending a spray in Avery's direction, and then he swam off a ways. Avery had just won a battle. Slipping back down in the water, he fumbled with the locks again and eventually got it open. He did his best not to let any water splash up and into the trunk, although that was largely a hopeless exercise.

Fumbling around, he felt leather, probably a portfolio, and then he felt something warm. He didn't dare tip the thing to look, for fear it would turn right over. So he gently felt until he got his hand under the fabric and pulled it out.

"A wool coat!" If he'd been given a million dollars, he couldn't have been happier. Very gingerly he lifted the coat up so it would rest on top of the open lid, and then he gently started closing the lid, all the time trying to keep the coat on top so that it wouldn't get wet. Just as he was about to close it, he had a thought and struck his hand deep inside. He found something fabric—he had no idea what—and gently pulled it out. Almost better than a coat, it turned out to be a sweater. Very gently he pushed that on top of the trunk, and then he closed and locked the lid. It was a watertight trunk, so closing it that way would successfully trap the air inside to maintain buoyancy.

All right, then, now all you've got to do is get yourself out of the water. It was hard, but eventually he got a leg up on the trunk and then reached an arm to the other side, slowly pulling himself on without managing to turn it over. As he lay on the trunk, he breathed heavily.

And then he sat up and pulled the wool coat on. The miraculous wool held in his body heat, the warmth instantaneous and wonderful. *If anything gives you a chance, this is it.* He looked at the horizon expectantly, figuring that it would be his luck that the rescue ship would show up just now, but it didn't.

Then he motioned to the man in the water. "Come on over! I think we can both manage it!" The fellow looked at him with hostile eyes. So Avery held up the wool sweater. "Come on! I'm sorry I was a sod. The worst that can happen is we both go tumbling in the water, and you're already there." It took a moment—pride and anger are powerful even when life itself is at stake—but ultimately the man started swimming to him. As he arrived, Avery motioned for him to go to the opposite end. He knew there was not enough room for both of them, but perhaps they could each put their torso on the trunk and leave just their legs in the water. At least that way the fellow wouldn't slip under the water from fatigue.

"Here. Put this on over what you've got, and then we'll reach across the trunk and take hands so we pull ourselves on easily." He went on to explain his thought about keeping themselves partially out of the water.

"Why are you doing this for me? I'm not sure I'd do it for you if the tables were reversed."

Avery shook his head. He wasn't really sure. "I guess because the tables could have been turned on us, and I could have been the one out in the water. I guess this is what I'd want you to do."

The fellow looked back at him through hollow eyes. By this point Avery had lowered his legs back into the water, and he reached out to take the man's hands. As he pulled the fellow up and partially out of the water, he laughed. "Why, you're as skinny as a rail! You couldn't have done a thing to me!" Somehow it pleased Avery immensely that the fellow chose to smile.

* * *

BY SIX PM THE SUN was still above the horizon, which was a godsend to those in the boats and water. Where the rays of the sun struck their skin, they felt warmth. It was illusory since many of the survivors were sunburned, which, with the salt water, caused them to be dehydrated and even more prone to suffering from the cold.

Another effect of three and a half hours in the water was that it was only the optimists who still looked toward the shore for rescuers. As one of these optimists, Ruth Jones was the first to call out, "Look, there's a boat! It's a much smaller boat than before. Perhaps the Germans won't want to torpedo it."

Hearing the sound of her voice woke Bill up from a short doze. Sitting up with a start, he rubbed his eyes and peered toward shore.

"It is a boat!" It was kind of hard to see since the little craft was plowing its way through the dark afternoon shadows, with the coast of Ireland even darker still.

"You men on the oars! Get them up there where they can see us!" shouted the lieutenant. Everyone on the boat knew this time it was real, since Lieutenant Ames stood up where he was and started waving.

"They are coming, aren't they?" asked Mrs. Jones.

"They are indeed. And the Germans certainly wouldn't waste a torpedo for a craft that size." Bill was almost a little embarrassed at how giddy his voice sounded, but he couldn't contain himself. "They are coming!"

The little boat made a turn in the water that brought it onto a heading directly aimed at their position, and someone came out to the front of the wheelhouse and started waving.

"They've spotted us for sure!" another yelled, and laughter broke out over the whole boat.

Bill drew a deep breath and then sat back down in his spot. A cold wave splashed him with water, as if to temper his happiness. As he raised his sleeve to wipe his face, he looked out in the water. Perhaps thirty feet away, a body was drifting facedown. Looking up beyond that, he could see that the relatively tight group of nearly a thousand who had started in the water had now dispersed into broken little clusters that extended beyond his line of sight.

"They'll have a hard time finding everyone after it gets dark." His heart ached as he realized that some who were still alive would die anyway, because the rescue boats wouldn't be able to find them. "Avery . . ." The name faded in the twilight as he wondered if his brother was out there. Would he be found? Was he alive?

Chapter 20

One by One

"I thought our little rescue boat would sink right in the water . . ." said Ruth Jones. The woman hadn't stopped talking since they got off the fishing boat in Queenstown. Meanwhile, Bill was nursing a cup of hot cocoa and trying to stay warm under a blanket. Some of the local women had come down to the piers to meet the survivors with sandwiches and warm drinks as they came ashore. "Did you hear what I said, Bill?"

Bill turned and nodded. "I heard you. It was unbelievable how many of us they managed to cram on their little fishing boat." After rescuing everyone in their lifeboat, the captain of the small steamer had worked his way through the water for nearly an hour, picking up as many of those in the water as he possibly could. When virtually every available space on the deck was occupied by a person, they had turned for the coast. Happily, dozens of other craft from Queenstown and Kinsale had also set out for the rescue and were still arriving at the scene. Some, upon reaching shore with a load of survivors, had immediately refueled and turned around to go right back into the cold, dark ocean.

"You seem very sad," said Ruth. "Aren't you glad we were rescued?"

"My brother was on the *Lusy*. He worked down in the boiler rooms . . ." His voice caught, and for the first time, hot tears streaked down his cheeks.

"I'm so sorry." Ruth was silent for a time. "Can you tell me what he looks like? Perhaps I could help you find him."

The woman was a marvel. One of the oldest passengers on the ship, her energy appeared boundless, and no matter how discouraging the circumstance, she tried to find something positive to say. Still, he couldn't quite bring himself to talk, so he just shook his head.

"I've been so insensitive. Working on the ship, you probably have many friends who you're worried about."

He nodded. "As a matter of fact, I do."

"Who were those fellows you asked about just as the ship went down?"

Now he rather wished that she would be quiet, but he also realized that being forced to talk was probably good for his mind. Otherwise his thoughts and fears would run away from him.

"The one was my supervisor, Mr. Todd. The other was a very good friend of mine from my church. We had spent time together in New York City." Bill felt his throat tighten. "He'd been hurt, so I'm not sure how well he could have coped with the icy waters."

This time Ruth Jones gave him room for silence. She even put her fragile little arm around Bill's shoulders as he wept quietly.

* * *

"Listen, I know this isn't the best place to get to know each other, but if we're going to die out here, I at least want to know your name."

The fellow with the dark, hollow eyes looked up at Avery. "James Trenyon. I'm from Connecticut."

"Avery Shafer from Liverpool. I'd offer to shake your hand, but we both might fall completely in the water." Trenyon almost smiled, although Avery had the feeling he didn't do that much smiling even in the best of circumstances. "Well. That's good. Pleased to meet you."

"Do you really think we're going to die?"

"I shouldn't have said that—I just couldn't think of any other way to strike up a conversation. I think there's still a chance we'll be rescued." He looked up at the sky and judged that it must be nearly 7:00 pm. "And we might even be alive if it happens soon enough." He put his hand down on his side and applied pressure to provide some relief from the pain.

They had seen some people being rescued a little earlier, but the place where Avery had landed when he was blown from the ship had placed him among the farthest out to sea. While he thought they would be visible to the rescue boats, the small rescue craft had filled up with people before they could get to Avery and Trenyon. When the light was finally gone, it would be very easy for the rescuers to miss them in the dark.

"I don't know how much longer I can hang on," said Trenyon. "I'm an accountant."

Avery laughed. Somehow that just seemed a very odd way to express that. "No offense intended. It's just that I'm a collier working with thousands of pounds of coal a day, and I'm not at all sure I can hold on. So I don't know that your being an accountant is a disadvantage."

"I'm not as strong as you . . ." Trenyon started to protest.

"But you don't have nearly as much body to hold up. I must weigh three times as much as you. Kind of wish I'd stayed away from some of those pork chops, now."

Trenyon finally did smile. "Ah, but if you do have any fat, which I doubt, at least it protects you from the cold. I have nothing but this sweater you gave me and some cotton pants."

"I know. This wool coat is better than nothing, but it's sucked up half the water in the Atlantic Ocean—it weighs nearly as much as I do."

Trenyon nodded but didn't say anything. Avery was very glad for the conversation, since he hated to be alone, at least in times of distress. He liked spending time alone reading, and he didn't mind the solitude of working with the boilers, since it gave him time to think about what he had read. But at the end of the day, he liked to recharge his batteries with conversation. He wasn't sure that was true of Trenyon.

"There's another one," Trenyon said evenly.

"Where?" asked Avery. He nearly lost his grip on the trunk when he craned his neck to look. He'd already fallen in a couple of times, as had Trenyon, and it was getting much more difficult to pull themselves back up with each incident.

"Over there."

Avery strained to see. "Where—it's a fishing boat!" Somehow he'd imagined himself being rescued by a battle cruiser. Instead, he saw a relatively small fishing boat with sails, manned by some burly Irish fishermen.

"Over here!" he shouted. "Over here!"

Realizing that there really was a chance of rescue, Trenyon even pulled himself further up on the trunk and raised his left arm into the air where he started waving.

"They've spotted us!" Trenyon shouted. He was the one who was facing the boat. "They're coming." He slumped back down in the water. "I really didn't think this would happen. I thought we'd die here." Trenyon's voice grew quieter. "In fact, I was just to the point of telling you good-bye."

"Good-bye? What does that mean? There's no place to go out here."

"You can go down."

"Oh." Avery swallowed hard, not knowing what to say to that.

* * *

BILL SLUMPED AGAINST THE ROCK wall in total exhaustion. It was now nearly midnight, and he'd been up and down the docks a dozen times looking for people he knew. He was always pleased when he saw one of his assigned passengers. But there was no sign of Avery or Everett. One lady swore that she had seen both Mr. Stringham and John Todd as he described them to her, but he hadn't been able to find them. Of course, it was certainly possible to miss them in the confusion. By now nearly eight hundred living survivors had been landed, some in terrible shape, and only now were boats returning filled with corpses. From the rows and rows of bodies being lined up on the sidewalks, it seemed certain there would be more dead than living.

Bill was assigned to sleep here, on the floor of the marketplace. Fortunately, the townspeople had provided him with a good blanket and some fresh straw to sleep on. There were dozens of other men with him. Feeling claustrophobic, he'd moved to a spot just outside the door. Even though he knew it was irrational, he couldn't bring himself to move inside.

"Bill. Bill!"

Startled, he looked up at Ruth Jones. *What now,* he thought. *Is there ever a time I don't have to be a Cunard employee?* He immediately felt guilty, knowing that Mrs. Jones had been out tirelessly trying to help people, including him.

"Yes, ma'am? What is it?"

She looked at him with kindly eyes. "I'm going to go to bed now. I wanted you to know that I haven't heard any news about your brother or friends."

"I haven't either." His voice sounded tired, even to him.

She sat down on a bench next to where he was sitting on the hay. "I'm not going to try to create any false hope for you. We both know that you may have lost all of them. But people are still arriving, and you can know for sure in the morning. In the meantime, I hope you can sleep."

A lump grew in his throat. He was so desperate to find Avery, but no more so than the hundreds of people who walked up and down the docks asking about a husband, a wife, a child, or a parent. The sounds of the dock were overwhelming. Some people were hysterical, others inconsolable, and still others would break out in unnatural laughter—so relieved to be safe that their emotions would simply spill out in all kinds of ways.

Bill looked up and took Mrs. Jones's hand. It struck him for the first time that perhaps she needed consoling, not for any lost ones—he knew that she was traveling by herself—but simply for going through the trauma of what they had experienced. She was strong and kind, but she was still human. "I'm sorry for what happened to you today. A person who's lived as well as you have shouldn't have to experience such violence."

Her voice caught for just a moment. "Thank you." She gulped and pretended to wipe some hair from her face. "It could have been so much worse. In the hotel where they've assigned me to stay, there is a woman who they thought was dead when they brought her on the rescue ship. They had laid her body out on the deck with the other corpses. But then a crewman of the rescue ship thought he saw a tear in her eye. They brought her to an inside cabin next to a stove where the men started rubbing her legs and arms as vigorously as they could. Eventually she started to revive, and they gave her blankets." She cleared her throat in embarrassment. "Apparently the poor dear was nearly naked when they pulled her from the water."

Bill nodded. "I feel sorriest for the men down in the boiler room. I saw a man who had worked with my brother . . ." He worked to steady his breathing. "He had terrible burns on his face and arms. He was standing under one of the steam lines when it burst. He looks terrible."

"Will he live?"

Bill shook his head. "I doubt it."

"Were you able to ask him about your brother?"

"I asked him, and he said he thought he saw him alive after the blast. But I'm not sure he's in any condition to know."

She nodded. "Well, as I say, no false hopes. But that doesn't mean there can't be any hope." She smiled and squeezed his hand. "You should come stay inside. I'm sure they'll make room for one more. It's getting cold out here."

The very thought of it filled him with panic. "No, that's all right. I'll be fine out here."

"Well, then, I need to go to bed. I'm not as young as I used to be."

Bill laughed. "No one would ever know." He stood up. "I'll walk you to your room."

"Of course. Thank you."

They heard another boat pull up to the dock as they started to walk toward the old hotel. Bill felt a surge of hope.

"Let's go look," she said.

"Okay. Just in case." They made their way through the small crowd that was gathering. It had now become almost a ritual—a new boat would show up, all those who had lost track of someone would gather, and then they'd make a corridor for the newly arrived survivors to pass through. As they did, there would sometimes be a gasp in the crowd. That's what had happened when a husband and wife stumbled into each other. They had both believed the other killed, and their reunion was overwhelming to watch. Now everyone hoped for such an outcome.

As one of the fellows dragged himself off, he stepped to the side of the crowd, right next to Bill and Mrs. Jones.

"Can I help you," she asked. He was fumbling in his pockets.

"It's my glasses. I just need to retrieve them from my pocket."

As he fumbled, he finally pulled out his crumpled glasses, still serviceable. They were wrapped in a piece of soggy paper. As he unfolded the paper, he shook his head in disbelief. "Would you look at this? It's the German Embassy warning posted in the *New York*

Times on the day we left port. It's warning us that we sail at our own risk."

Mrs. Jones clicked her tongue as Bill shook his head. Almost no one had taken the warning seriously, and now the ship was on the bottom of the ocean. The fellow remarked, "Well, at least I have one souvenir of the day's events."

"That's the last of them," said Bill dejectedly.

"Perhaps tomorrow."

Bill could not imagine tomorrow.

* * *

"WE'RE FINALLY HERE," SAID THE old fisherman. "Sorry it took us so long."

Avery had been shivering again, for perhaps the past half hour. The wind had fallen off, and so the sailboat had waited idle a few miles offshore. The fishermen had taken to rowing to make some progress, but even with that it had taken much longer than expected, and they had put in at the village of Kinsale, rather than continuing on to Queenstown. Still, Avery managed to say thank-you to his rescuers as they tied the boat to the shore. They merely shrugged. A seaside village such as this was used to disasters, the villagers used to risking their lives to save those in distress.

As Avery tried to stand up, he cried out in pain, and his legs buckled beneath him. The pain that shot through his side almost made him pass out. He'd successfully ignored his injury while in the water; perhaps, in part, because of the cold, but almost certainly because he'd had far more important things to worry about. Or perhaps he was in shock. But now he couldn't ignore the pain.

"What is it?"

"My side. I may have broken my ribs, although it seems deeper than that. It's much worse now that I've been sitting." He gingerly made his way back to the bench he'd been sitting on. "Maybe if I just sit here a bit."

"We'll come back for you."

He watched as they leaned down to pick James Trenyon up. "Is he going to be all right?" Avery simply couldn't trust his own judgment. James Trenyon was quite still in the boat. During the hours at sea, he too had shivered as they were rescued but then had gone quiet and still. People had tried to rouse him but to no avail.

"If you believe in heaven, then he's doing very well right now."

Avery nodded. He was embarrassed to stifle a small sob. "I didn't know him. We just met on our little raft." The men nodded. "He was an accountant!" Avery blurted out, realizing that it was a foolish thing to say. But it had mattered to Trenyon. After that, he couldn't say anything more. Fortunately, these men were very austere, and they didn't press. He watched in silence as they removed the body from the boat, placing it in the back of a wagon that had been left there by the locals who had stayed up as late as they could.

Coming back on the boat, the elder in the group said, "Come on, then. Let's get you something warm to drink and then to the doctor."

"I'll be all right." But when Avery tried to stand up a second time, he passed out on the spot.

Chapter 21
Survivors and Victims

Liverpool, England

The knock on the door startled Clara Shafer nearly out of her wits. Jumping from her rocking chair with a start, she was overwhelmed by the simultaneous surge of hope and dread. Ever since she'd heard of the sinking of the *Lusitania,* she'd been terrified at the thought of both of her boys having possibly drowned.

Before she could reach the door, there was a second, even more urgent knock. Still, Clara was a deliberate woman and opened the door just a crack.

"Oh, Mary . . . it's you!" Clara threw the door open and received the distraught Mary Winnel into her arms, where the two women just hugged while tears streaked down their faces.

"Where's Frankie?" said Clara, finally breaking their embrace.

Mary stepped back and wiped her face with her white apron. "He's with a neighbor. Do you think . . . do you think . . ."

"I think that my boys are fine." Clara took a couple of deep breaths to steady herself. "We've both been through this before, so we know what the worst that can happen is. But we need to have faith that they are in God's hands and that wherever they are, He will care for them."

Mary nodded slowly, her mouth trembling as she did so. Finally the reserve gave way. "Oh, I don't know what I'll do. My heart can't take this again." Clara stepped forward and embraced her once again.

* * *

Queenstown, Ireland

THE SCENE ON THE QUEENSTOWN docks the next morning was unique in history. While there had been many a boat wreck on the Irish coast, never had they experienced anything on this scale. The loss of life was catastrophic—likely to approach the number who perished on the *Titanic* three years earlier. The sinking of the *Titanic,* though, had been an accident between a ship and an iceberg—perhaps the result of incompetence, but an accident nonetheless. This was premeditated murder, and newspapers the world over howled in indignation. German immigrant–owned stores were already being looted in Liverpool; angry crowds had gathered in Washington, DC, demanding a response from the Wilson administration; and the Admiralty in London was dispatching a score of bureaucrats to Ireland while moving quickly to suppress the history of their abysmally incompetent correspondence with the *Lusitania* in the days leading up to the sinking.

But all of that was of little meaning to the people in Queenstown. They were desperate to find their loved ones, a task that required they go back and forth in the streets looking for one another. Then, as they had the strength to face it, a trip to the improvised morgue that the coroner had set up. Bill and the other survivors who were looking for their loved ones had to pass by hundreds of bodies laid out in row after row, the bodies already starting to putrefy in the relatively warm spring air. Some of the corpses were disfigured by injury, others by the pained expressions on their faces as they died, and still others were merely the remains of shattered bodies that no one could recognize. The coroner was efficient, fully grasping the urgent task before him. He had enlisted a small army of volunteers to go up and down the rows examining the bodies while writing as complete a description as they could so that their survivors could later identify them. Any personal items were carefully noted and preserved, since that would be yet another way to give families some sense of closure.

Bill had just been up and down the rows, not finding any of those whom he sought.

So he'd walked to the center of the dock. "Have you seen a man with brown hair . . . quite stocky . . . he worked in the boiler rooms? His name is Avery Shafer."

The frazzled Cunard clerk shook his head. "Sorry."

"What about a passenger named Stringham? Everett Stringham. He was in first class." Bill added that last part, since it was likely that Cunard would take more care to communicate the fate of their first-class passengers. But the man shook his head again. "Sorry. No one with that name."

Bill sighed, and the fellow finally looked up. "I'm sorry, I really am. But there are so many . . ."

Bill nodded. "I understand. I'll keep looking.

It still wasn't out of the question that someone was alive. Even now boats were arriving at the docks, although there were very few survivors among the bodies coming off. Which is why he knew he'd have to go back to the morgue time and again. Of course there was a chance that Avery had gone down inside the ship, but Bill wasn't ready to face that thought just yet.

"Any word?" asked a feminine voice. He turned and saw his guardian angel coming up to him.

"Good morning, Mrs. Jones." He shrugged and shook his head.

"Have you had anything to eat?"

Bill tried to remember. "Some coffee—that's all they had, and I was very cold."

She raised a curious eyebrow but didn't ask why that would be a concern.

"I've found a little café down the street. Would you let me buy you lunch?"

"I really should check the morgue . . ." She didn't try to stop him, but she also held his gaze as if to encourage him to take a rest from it. "Why, sure. I'd like that. But you don't need to buy." In the act of saying that, he felt inside his pockets and realized that whatever money he'd had was now six or seven hundred feet beneath the surface of the ocean.

She watched as he went through this exercise. "I managed to keep a small purse through all we experienced, so it will be my treat."

Once again he walked with her through the lonesome streets of Queenstown. One could immediately tell who the survivors of the wreck were, inasmuch as they were mostly wearing clothing that didn't fit—donated by the townspeople—or clothing that was torn and wrinkled from hours in the water. Many had an almost zombie-like look on their faces, while others reacted nervously to any sort of unexpected noise or commotion.

Once inside the pub, Ruth ordered a glass of hot chocolate for Bill, having observed his habit. Unfortunately, they had none. "Maybe some hot water," he said.

"And bring us both one of those bowls of creamed soup," she said. "And a ham sandwich on that marvelous bread."

After they had gotten their food and were seated, Ruth said, "Now tell me about your brother and friends. What were they like?"

Bill swallowed hard and then thought back to all the good times with his brother, growing up in Liverpool together, and to his brief friendship with Everett Stringham.

* * *

EVERETT WAS NEARLY FROZEN WHEN they plucked him from the table. John Todd had slipped off and into the water hours before, his corpse sinking silently beneath the waves. Everett had wept until he was all out of tears. Then he had shivered in the cold until he lost consciousness. He still wasn't clear how the boat had found him—perhaps because the table he was on was painted white, which probably stood out in the moonlight.

Now, as they were pulling into port in the late morning, he realized that he might live, after all. He'd doubted it the night before, even after being rescued. But now the sun shone on his neck and back, and he enjoyed the warmth.

"Thank you for saving me."

"It's the least we could do," said the old fisherman kindly, "after what all of you have been through. We've seen our share of wrecks in these waters, but nothing to compare to this." Pointing to a shack down the street, the fisherman said, "Make your way there—the Cunard people will make arrangements for you."

Everett extended his hand and then simply stepped forward and put his arms around the man's neck. "Thank you for my life."

* * *

Bill found his conversation with Ruth very comforting in the midst of all this uncertainty. As they walked along, Bill actually forgot that he would need to go back to the morgue. It had been good to have an hour pass speaking of faith and hope, of friends and family.

"Where will you go now?" he asked.

"On to Scotland, I suppose. I was going over there to visit a cousin. My mother immigrated to America and never saw her sister again. Just before she died, she extracted a promise from me that I would find her sister's grave and pay her respects." She looked out to sea for a moment. "And now I've got to face getting on another ship."

"Kind of frightening, isn't it?"

Without really consciously setting out for the Cunard office, Bill soon found that he had led them there.

"Go ahead and check. Perhaps something has turned up," Ruth suggested.

"Come in with me."

She assented, and they went back to the clerk who had tried to brush Bill off earlier.

"Excuse me, but I was inquiring after Avery Shafer or Everett Stringham . . ."

Without so much as looking up, the clerk said, "I told you earlier that I haven't heard anything. We'll notify you when we do."

"I was just thinking . . ."

"We'll notify you!"

As Bill turned to leave, another clerk two tables over spoke up. "Did you say Shafer?"

"Yes, Avery Shafer. He worked in the boiler room. He's my brother . . ."

The new clerk looked over at him. "I just got a telegram from Kinsale. It's about thirty miles down the bay. It says that they picked your brother up last night and that we were to notify you, if you could be found. He's been injured and can't be moved right now."

Bill became dizzy where he stood. "Injured? How badly? What's wrong with him?" It was amazing how fast his mind moved from "Is he alive" to "Is he all right?"

The clerk stood up and walked over to him. "Hold on there . . . it's a telegram, not a medical history. Just, 'Avery Shafer, alive, injured.

Notify Bill Shafer, brother. Cannot be moved.' I'm afraid I don't know any more than that."

"Injured. But at least he's alive!" Bill was agitated now. "How do I get there?"

"By boat, usually. But nothing's going out." The fellow walked out front, with Bill and Ruth following. "Wait a minute. Maybe . . ." He motioned for them to stay put while he jogged over to a large wagon that was being loaded with some lime. Finally the clerk trotted back over to them. "That fellow is going down to Kinsale. They need lime for the bodies they have to deal with. He says you can ride with him if you can go right now. It should take four or five hours to get there. A boat would be faster, but I don't know when one will go that direction."

"I'm ready," replied Bill.

The clerk smiled at him. "Then go jump on the wagon. I'm glad your brother's alive. I hope he isn't injured too badly."

"Thank you! Thank you!" He turned to Ruth. "He's alive. Avery somehow made it!"

She allowed him to take her hands into his as he moved restlessly. "I'll have to get a telegram off to Mum. She'll be worried sick until I do." He looked around nervously, knowing that he wouldn't have time before he had to leave on the wagon. "It doesn't seem right to wait until I get there, but I suppose it will be better to tell her everything once I learn more about Avery."

"Why don't you let me send the telegram?" She fumbled in her purse and pulled out a piece of paper and pencil. "Write your mother's name and address, and I'll tell her what we know."

"Oh, Ruth. That would be so wonderful." He felt in his pockets for money, forgetting that he was penniless.

"It's all right. I need to do something positive, particularly since you'll be leaving me."

"How can I ever repay you?"

"Send me a letter telling me how you and your brother turn out. That will be thanks enough." She handed him a beautifully printed card with her name and address on it.

Impulsively Bill leaned down and kissed her on the cheek. "Thank you. I don't know what I'd have done without you." She smiled, although it looked as if she might cry. Bill wanted to stay, but he had to go. "Good-bye, then." He turned, hesitated, and then added, "Please add, 'Tell Mary,' at the end of the telegram. Mum will know what it means."

Ruth nodded, and Bill jumped into the back of the wagon. "Thank you," he called as they disappeared around a corner.

Turning on the street, Ruth started her way back to her hotel. As she did so, she accidentally bumped into a very distinguished man with a hurt arm.

"Pardon me," she said.

Even though he was obviously cold and hurting, he immediately stopped and apologized. Nodding, she started off again. But something caught her attention—his American accent, perhaps, or his eyes.

"Excuse me!" she called out to him. The man turned at her call. "You don't happen to be Everett Stringham, do you?"

The surprised look on his face made it clear that he was. "How did you know that?" he started to say, just as Ruth said, "Oh, dear, and Bill is gone . . ." It was one of those impossible coincidences that seemed to be happening all up and down the pier. Ruth moved forward to him. "You're hurt. I need to help you."

"But why . . . I don't know who you are."

"We have a common friend," said Ruth. "A very good young man who has been worried sick about you. And now he's off to find his brother, who has also been reported alive."

"Bill?" Everett Stringham was overjoyed to learn that his friend was still alive.

* * *

BILL BURST INTO THE LITTLE hospital in the village of Kinsale, almost knocking the town's only doctor over as he did so.

"Sorry. My brother, Avery Shafer . . . ?"

"He's in there. He's asleep right now."

"Can I see him?"

"Sure. But he's not doing so well. It seems as if he had some ribs broken, and it's caused some internal bleeding. There was a lot of trauma. I'm not a surgeon, but I've done my best."

"So, he'll be all right?"

The doctor stared at the floor for a moment. "I think it may have hit his kidney. If so, he could be in for some troubled days."

"His kidney? What does that mean?"

"Well, fortunately we all have two kidneys, so his body can continue to process waste. But once he got stabilized, he threw up a fair amount of blood. If that keeps up, he'll have to have surgery."

"Where?"

The doctor shook his head. "Not here. Even if we could get a surgeon to come down, he'd be appalled at our lack of facilities. If worse comes to worst, we'll have to move him to Queenstown. But it would be incredibly painful."

"Where do you feel kidney pain?" Bill wondered if he was asking all these questions just to avoid going in and seeing Avery. His brother was always the tough, healthy one.

"Flank pain." The doctor reached out and grabbed Bill's skin on the right side of his back, just above his hip and directly below his rib cage.

"Ow!"

"There you are. Imagine a pain deep inside your body that hurts so bad that you want to cry. Patients with kidney problems twist and turn, hoping that by changing position they can take the pressure off and find some relief. But it isn't related to pressure, and so it doesn't work. It's just a vital organ in spasms because of the trauma it has suffered."

"But it's not life-threatening?"

"I said that his other kidney can process waste. But you can't just go on bleeding inside your body. That can kill you just as well as bleeding on the outside.

"We'll have to watch him very carefully over the next twelve hours. If he continues to vomit blood, we'll have to do something. Hopefully it will seal up on its own, and then he can start the recovery process."

"How long does that take?"

The doctor shook his head, exasperated. "As long as it wants to. About two weeks of bed rest, minimum. As I said, in even the best of circumstances, it's painful, and with everything else he's been through, it will be even worse."

Bill inhaled slowly and let it out in a long, sustained sigh. "Thank you. I'm sorry I asked so many questions, but he's never been sick. So all this is new to me."

"Were you on the *Lusitania*?"

Bill nodded. "I was lucky enough to be on an upper deck. We both work for Cunard, so I was enlisted to help with a lifeboat. I made it away with no injuries." He swallowed hard. So many people hadn't made it. Or were terribly injured.

"Well, why don't you go sit with your brother. I've got a lot of injured people to take care of—to say nothing of filling in for the coroner until he gets here. But if you need me, just come out to the porch and call. I'll come running."

Bill shook the doctor's hand and then moved inside the small, dark room where Avery was sleeping. The bed was too small for him. When he drew closer, Bill was startled at how pale Avery's face was. Rather than startle him, he gently picked up a wooden chair and set it down right next to the bed. Sitting down, Bill tried to sort through the thousands of thoughts that filled his mind. Bill sat up sharply when Avery stirred, ready to put his hand out if he needed to be calmed down. But his brother simply groaned in his sleep and shifted slightly in the bed. Eventually Bill laid his head on the sheet next to him and in a matter of moments was lost in deep slumber.

* * *

"Surface. We need to report in."

"Yes, sir. Surface!" Lanz waited until the ship broke the surface and then quickly mounted the ladder to the conning tower, where he opened the hatch. The wave of rank, putrid air that swept up and out of the ship was quickly replaced by a wonderful breeze of fresh ocean air. "All clear!"

Once he saw that the deck crew was out and properly seeing to their routine, which included checking the deck gun, scouring the deck for any debris, etc., Lanz slid back down the rail into the cabin.

Schweiger was smiling. "We've been ordered to Emden. And then I am to go to Berlin to meet with officers at the highest level! The Kaiser himself has congratulated us, and the newspapers and radio broadcasts are celebrating our triumph. They assumed it was us who sank the *Lusitania,* but now that we have confirmed it, we are being hailed as heroes."

"Congratulations, sir."

Schweiger grew serious. “Even though I will be the one wined and dined, you know that you were crucial to our success. In the moment of crisis, you stepped in and made sure that my orders were obeyed.”

“My duty. But I am glad I was there.”

“I think I’ll go on top. This may prove to be a very good thing for Germany. If the Kaiser is pleased, then it must serve his purposes.”

As the captain disappeared up the ladder, Lanz looked after him with mixed emotions. “I doubt there is much rejoicing in England or America.”

* * *

AS THE DAYS PASSED BY, many of the residents of Queenstown were surprised at the continuing shock that registered in the vacant expressions on the faces of survivors. A handful had continued on their journey to England. Some reports claimed they all refused to take off their life jackets, even while traveling on a train. Others continued to go up and down the coast looking for loved ones whose bodies may have washed ashore, and still others simply did not have the will to move on. The mayor had scheduled a mass burial with a large funeral service, hoping that would help some of the victims deal with their emotions.

Still, there were some who were more resilient and compassionate, including Ruth Jones, while others were clearly angry. To those who knew him, Captain Turner still seemed to be in shock. For example, he’d knelt and wept when he saw one of his bridge officers lying prostrate in the morgue, which was highly uncharacteristic for such a taciturn man. Other times he was oddly detached.

In one case, a young man yelled at the captain, “You there, Captain Turner! What do you have to say for yourself?”

After not receiving a response, the young man said, “I asked you a question!” The man was dressed in such a way that placed him as a third-class passenger. When he grabbed at Turner’s sleeve, the captain turned on him with a rather vacant expression.

“It is the fortunes of war,” was all he said, with such calm that it disarmed his accuser. Turner sighed and pulled his sleeve loose, continuing on his way. It was the first of many accusers he would face in the days and months ahead.

By now, Ruth Jones had become a common fixture in Queenstown, offering aid and comfort to those who seemed to be lost or alone. She visited Everett in the little hospital, where he had spent the first two days mostly asleep. Between his injured ribs, broken arm, and the other trauma he'd faced, he was in desperate need of rest. Ruth had sent a telegram to Kinsale telling Bill that he was alive. She understood when all she received in return was a two-word telegram that said, "Thank you." Bill simply didn't have a lot of money for telegrams.

Sometimes she did her small part to help the world by buying someone a sandwich or hot drink at her favorite restaurant while listening to their story. It was amazing how desperately people needed to tell their individual stories of the sinking and ordeal in the water and ultimate rescue over and over again. It's in the retelling that the human mind finally comes to accept what at first seems impossible. On this occasion, she was listening to a young woman named Nan Williams who had worked in the kitchen and who very nearly got on the elevator that later trapped so many in a cage of death. Nan was not among those with the vacant stares.

The girl glanced up from the newspaper that Ruth had purchased earlier that day. "It's hard to believe all these riots taking place all around the world. I knew the *Lusitania* was important, but I had no idea people cared this much."

"It's the first time in history that a civilized nation has so blatantly attacked a civilian ship. I don't know where it will all stop." Ruth took a sip of her drink. "The poor man at the Cunard office told me that their offices in London, Liverpool, and New York are being mobbed by hysterical people wanting to know if their relative or friend is alive. The answer depends on what has been discovered here, and the clerks are absolutely overwhelmed by trying to sort out the living from the missing and the dead. I feel quite sorry for them."

"I don't. Cunard should have protected us. Instead they sailed us right into the path of that submarine. I put my life in their hands, and see how they treated me."

Ruth turned back to her paper. She was out to offer comfort, not recriminations. "Oh, dear. It says here that Mr. Vanderbilt's wife, Margaret, has locked herself in her suite at the Vanderbilt Hotel while his mother is in their mansion praying that he is alive. Apparently they plan to offer a $5,000 reward for anyone who finds him or his body."

"Really, $5,000? That's a fortune! What could I do with $5,000?"

"I don't think they'll find him. I actually saw him as I was getting into the lifeboat. He was very gallant, helping people with their life jackets and calmly pointing them to the nearest lifeboat. I even saw him take off his own life jacket and put it on a child. He was in every way a gentleman, and I believe that cost him his life."

"Perhaps they won't find him, but I'll wager people will scour the coast for weeks trying. A reward that size is almost irresistible."

At that moment, Ruth nearly lost her hearing as Nan let out a shriek of joy. "It's Barbara!" She jumped up from the table, knocking her chair down as she did, and raced out the door to where Ruth observed her hugging another girl about her same age. Ruth took up her cup and sipped on the soothing liquid.

"Good," she said while setting the cup down. "At least she has someone to share this with now." She continued to read in the paper about the anti-German riots breaking out on every continent in the world. Right here in Queenstown, the proprietor of the Queen's Hotel, a man named Otto Humbert, was said to have spent the first night hiding in the basement of the hotel for fear of someone beating him because he was German.

"It was awful, but I fear it will cause even more violence. That will be the greatest tragedy." Ruth found that she couldn't pick up her cup because of the wave of grief that swept over her.

* * *

Evanston, Wyoming

Annie Stringham sat on her porch. Late May isn't really warm enough for that, but there she was, with only a shawl.

"What are you going to do?"

Annie turned to her sister, Maggie, who had come out of the house two times previously to encourage her to come inside where it was warm. But not this time.

"I want to go to England to rescue him," she replied. "But that's too dangerous." She struggled with a knot that she'd been tying and untying since finally receiving a telegram informing her that Everett was alive but injured. "I want him to come home, but perhaps even that's too dangerous. I just hope that people there can take care of him."

"I'm sure they can. From what I read in the newspaper, the people of Queenstown are magnificent in what they're doing for the survivors."

"I'm just so grateful . . . that he's . . . a survivor." With that, Annie started weeping. There were so many who were not. While most of the world could only imagine what it was like on the *Lusitania,* Annie had been on board just a few weeks earlier. It was easy for her to picture all the many people who had died. She would never feel entirely safe again.

Chapter 22
Recriminations

Bill jerked awake as the nightmare reached a particularly disturbing scene. He was frightened that he didn't know where he was.

Avery said quietly, "Hey there, little brother, you made it. I'm glad you're here."

Bill straightened up in the chair next to Avery's bed and yawned. "How long have I been asleep?"

"I don't know, because I was asleep for most of it myself. I've been awake about five minutes is all."

Bill reached for his pocket watch, a gift from his father, but realized that he had left it in his quarters. It had gone to the bottom of the ocean with the *Lusitania*.

He rubbed his eyes to clear them and then turned to Avery. "I'm glad you made it, too. I was kind of frantic, particularly when I couldn't find you at Queenstown."

"I think we were the last ones in. A sailboat without wind isn't very fast." He tried to smile, but Bill could see how much pain he was in.

"So what happened to your kidney? The doctor says you've made a mess of it or something."

Usually Avery would have a witty or sarcastic reply, but this time he responded directly to the question. "I don't know for sure. I think I must have been thrown against something when the torpedo hit. To tell you the truth, I was so darn scared I didn't pay much attention. Then when I got blasted out to sea, I'm sure that added to it."

"Blasted?"

Avery turned and smiled. "You won't believe my story. I doubt anyone will. But it is as true as possible."

"So tell me—my story's kind of boring. I was on my way to find Mr. Stringham when they called me over to help with a lifeboat. We got it loaded and lowered, and we were in the water for three or four hours before being rescued. There were some awful things, but nothing really bad for me." He paused. "Or exciting, like getting blasted . . ."

Avery twisted in the bed, trying to find a way to get comfortable. "All right, then, let me tell you the adventure of escaping from below the waterline." For the next twenty minutes, Avery did his best to describe everything that happened—the terror of being in the boiler room and hearing and feeling the blast go off . . . how disoriented he'd been losing his hearing. He almost broke down when telling about the people in the elevator and then described the total shock of being blown clear off the funnel. "And now I find out that I'm bleeding inside. That's a little more adventure than I would have hoped for."

"The doctor says they may have to do surgery."

"You know, I hate the thought of a knife and would usually tell them to shove off and leave me alone. But this time is different. They've got to do something for this pain. For a while I was afraid I was going to die from it, and then I was afraid I wouldn't die."

Bill put his hand on Avery's arm. "It's rotten that this has happened to you, but I'm just so glad you're alive. A friend of mine sent a telegram to Mum, so at least she knows we're both here."

Avery nodded. "That's good." His body tensed up, and he let out an involuntary gasp.

"What is it?"

Avery answered through clenched teeth. "Spasms. They come every so often, and it makes it so I can hardly breathe."

"Let me get the doctor. He told me to call him if you need something." He half expected Avery the tough guy to decline the offer and felt bad when he just nodded.

"Right, then I'll be off." As he made his way to the front porch, he found the doctor as well as a policeman. "My brother. He's having spasms or something. He needs you."

"I'll go see him. I can give him some laudanum to calm his nerves, but we have to watch that. It's a narcotic, you know." Bill started to turn to follow the doctor when he was interrupted by the policeman.

"Begging your pardon, but is your name William Shafer?"

Bill hesitated, a feeling of dread coming over him. "Yes, sir. People call me Bill." His mind raced—did this have something to do with Mr. Stringham, with Ruth? She'd said that Everett was all right.

"Good. I'm here on behalf of the Cork County coroner." Now Bill was certain it was bad news. "It seems that he's convening an inquest this afternoon, right here in Kinsale. He believes it's his responsibility to determine responsibility for all these deaths. So by virtue of his authority as the coroner on the scene, he's summoned Captain Turner of the *Lusitania* to come testify. It was suggested by one of the officers that you could be called as a reliable witness . . ."

"Me? A witness in an inquest?"

"Not to worry. Everyone knows that you're an innocent party. The coroner just wants to find out what happened. He can't sign a bunch of death certificates without first examining the facts before him."

Bill chewed on his lower lip. He wasn't the type to enjoy standing in front of a group. But someone needed to help determine what happened. "I'll come. They can ask me anything they want."

The policeman nodded. "Very good. I'll put your name on the list. That doesn't mean you'll necessarily be called, but at least they'll know you're willing."

"Okay." Bill took a deep breath to buck up his courage. "Well, I better go to my brother."

When he got inside, his heart dropped as he saw Avery vomiting blood into a basin by the side of his bed, pain contorting his face.

"Can't you do something for him?" Bill asked the doctor.

"I've sent my assistant to send a telegram for a surgeon to come down posthaste. He should get here by 6:00 PM tonight. Normally we wouldn't operate without daylight, but this won't wait."

Avery finally got control and lay back in his bed. He looked up at Bill weakly. "I won't let myself die—not after everything I went through to get off that boat alive and survive the ocean."

Bill quickly swept a tear off his cheek. "Of course you won't. I'd give you one of my kidneys if I could."

"Oh, that's rich. People giving each other their kidneys."

"It was just an expression," said Bill defensively. "To show I love you, although I'm not sure why."

"It's all right, Bill. I know you're worried. But I mean it. I'm going to beat this. And this doctor here is going to save me."

"The surgeon will save you. I've just got to keep you alive until he gets here."

"Like I said, he'll save me." Avery allowed the doctor to give him a small drink of water. "Now, who was that you were talking to?"

"A policeman. They want me to testify at a coroner's inquest this afternoon. Captain Turner's going to testify as well. But I won't go to it now that you need surgery."

Avery struggled to sit up but couldn't muster the strength. "Of course you WILL testify. You can't do the surgery. Besides, it won't happen until after the inquest is over. You've got to tell the story. The world has to hear what happened to us." Avery started coughing again.

"It's all right. I'll testify, then." More quietly to the doctor, "But you'll send for me if you need to?"

"Of course."

With that, Bill went back to the chair by Avery's bed and pondered the events of the past two days as his brother fell back asleep.

* * *

BILL WAS NOT AMONG THOSE on the witness list who were called to testify, but he was able to sit in on the session where Captain Turner was the most prominent witness. When the session was concluded, he made straight for the hospital to be there for Avery's surgery. Stepping inside the waiting room, Bill was motioned by the local doctor to come over.

"It's good you showed up. We need you."

"Need me? For what—I'm not a medic."

"No, but I have to assist with the surgery, and the surgeon has to perform it. So we need you to aid with the administration of ether to put and keep your brother asleep. It's vital that he not wake during the procedure. Can you do that?"

Bill's head spun, almost as if he had vertigo. The thought of watching an operation, let alone helping in it, was disturbing. "Don't you have anyone else who is experienced? Like a nurse?"

The doctor shook his head. "Everyone is occupied. We'll tell you what to do—you don't need to worry."

Bill took a deep breath. "All right. Show me what to do." The doctor grabbed his arm and took him to a sink to wash his hands. Then he led him into the room where Avery was laid out on a bare table, with most of his body covered by sheets, except where the surgery was to take place. "How you doing?" asked Bill lamely.

"Not as well as I might be. The doctor says you're going to help with the operation."

"Shows just how desperate a situation you're in, doesn't it?" Bill tried to smile, but he was too frightened.

Avery rolled his head back and looked straight up at him. "It'll be all right, whatever happens. It won't be your fault if something goes wrong, so just do what they tell you."

"They tell me I'll be putting you to sleep."

"And I'll be grateful for that. Anything to make this pain go away." Bill couldn't help but notice how red Avery's eyes were. He was a tough character, and Bill imagined that anyone else would have been screaming in pain.

"Okay, then," said the surgeon. "Let's get started." He handed Bill a dark brown bottle of liquid. "Take the cap off and cover the opening with this cotton cloth. Tip the bottle upside-down so that some liquid seeps into the cloth. Then put the bottle down with the lid on—we don't want vapors escaping out into the room and putting us under." If it was an attempt at humor, Bill didn't laugh. He was way too nervous for that. But he did as he was told. "I want you to hold the side of the cloth that isn't saturated close to your brother's mouth and nose. Be careful not to have the liquid come into direct contact with the skin as it will burn him. He just needs to sniff enough vapors to lose consciousness. Then, throughout the surgery, we'll tell you to administer more if he starts to stir. But not too much, or it could suppress all bodily functions."

"What does that mean?" asked Bill in alarm.

"Just what it sounds like," the surgeon replied. "But don't worry, we'll be watching you."

"Are you ready?" Bill asked Avery.

"A little scared, but go ahead." He hesitated a moment. "And if something goes wrong, tell Mum I love her, and I'm sorry for anything I did to hurt her feelings."

Bill swallowed hard and then held the cloth in front of Avery's nose and mouth. Soon his brother was out cold, and the surgeon started his work.

* * *

"I'll give a deposition," said Everett, "although I doubt I can add much to the record."

"We just want to know whatever it is that you know. People you might have seen who aren't accounted for. The behavior of the ship's crew. Things like that. The whole world is watching us, and we need to get this down while it's fresh."

"I understand." Everett leaned back in his bed. It was a perfectly reasonable request by Cunard representatives. And yet the thought of living through the horror again was intimidating.

"Is there anyone in particular whom you can tell us about?"

"No—it was all so disordered." Everett closed his eyes and let his mind wander back. Surprisingly, the place it took him was to the slap he'd received on his face while lying unconscious in the entry to his cabin. Opening his eyes, he said quietly, "I guess I do have something to add to the record. I'd like to tell you about the man who saved my life. He was a chief steward, and it's because of him that I am here. His name was Todd—John Todd."

Then Everett began to tell the story of his last hour on the ship. What happened in the dark alley that night in New York City would never be recorded.

* * *

While looking back on the surgery hours later while waiting for Avery to wake up, Bill was startled when the doctor came in. "Still sleeping?"

Bill nodded. "Is that bad? Did I give him too much ether?"

"No. You did fine. There was that one time he started to come to, which was a little dicey given the spot we were in, but you took care of it."

"It looks like his face is red around his mouth. I tried not to let the ether have any direct contact. I feel terrible to think . . ."

"You shouldn't feel anything of the kind. You did as well as you could—I couldn't have done better myself. Besides, the surgery worked out, and I'm confident he'll recover well, although I'm not sure he'll ever have full use of that kidney. The damage was much worse than I expected, quite surprising given how little external trauma there was. He must have been thrown with a great deal of violence."

"He really is lucky to be alive. I heard one of the officers talking yesterday, and he said that only a handful of men from the boiler rooms have been accounted for. The majority probably went down with the ship."

"I have to go for a while," said the doctor. "My family hasn't seen me for three days. Let me tell you what to tell him when he wakes up and what to watch for that will prompt you to come get me." The doctor then proceeded to describe the tear in Avery's kidney and surrounding tissue and how the surgeon had been forced to remove a piece in order to get a clean line for stitching. But with everything put back together now, he should recover, although he might never be able to do the heavy lifting that was required by his job. The wound was left open intentionally so that the local doctor could remove the stitches when the time came, and then he would suture the incision on the outside.

"So what you want to do is give him confidence. Will you be able to stay with him?"

"Of course I will. My contract with Cunard had already ended, and I won't sign a new one until he's better. Maybe I won't sign at all."

"Scared of going back to sea? It wouldn't be a sign of weakness."

Bill shook his head. "A little, but that's not the reason. After all this, I think I should join the navy. What the Germans did to us must be stopped."

"A brave man. Well, it's an honorable thing to do. I guess you heard that the coroner ruled the deaths a homicide, with an indictment for the officers of the submarine."

"I did hear that. He even indicted the Kaiser." Bill shook his head. "Together they killed more than 1,200 men, women, and children. You wonder how they can call themselves a civilized nation."

* * *

CAPTAIN SCHWEIGER PAUSED IN FRONT of the restroom mirror to make certain his uniform was perfect. Running his fingers through his hair one last time, he stepped out into the marble corridor and started ascending the steps that would take him to meet with the admirals who prosecuted the war on behalf of Germany. Coming from a prominent Berlin family, he was not intimidated by men of power, but this was a unique day—an opportunity to be commended for the most spectacular show of German power in the war thus far. After all, he held in his hand the telegram he had received from Admiral Pohl within hours of the sinking. He still treasured the words:

"My highest appreciation of commander and crew for success achieved of which the High Seas Fleet is proud and my congratulations on their return."

He'd also been given copies of newspaper articles in which the German press had firmly placed the blame for the incident on the British, with one declaring that "hundreds of nonparticipant passengers were victims, victims of the haughty greed of English shipping lines," while others decreed that it was justified retribution for the British blockade that was attempting to starve thousands. A medallion in honor of the event had even been struck, showing the *Lusitania* listing to starboard. Little wonder that Schweiger was excited. As he reached the top of the stairs, he saw one of the general staff approaching him, an admiral by rank.

"Schweiger!"

The young captain snapped to attention. "Sir!"

"What are you doing here?" The tone was very nasty.

Shaken, Schweiger replied, "I was told to report here. To receive recognition for our last voyage." He was careful not to single out the sinking of the *Lusitania*.

"Recognition! For sinking a passenger liner? Certainly you must know the awful weight of criticism your foolish action has brought down on us in the world press. Some have even resorted to calling the Kaiser a murderer and a butcher . . ."

"But I was just following orders." Schweiger's face burned at the rebuke. "I was told to sink all enemy shipping, without restriction."

"Yes, but to shoot without warning?" The admiral shook his head. "It is a sad day when we find ourselves condemned the world over. The United States has even sent a highly critical memorandum demanding an apology and reparations. Can you imagine the Kaiser having to issue an apology?"

Schweiger swallowed hard, the bile in his throat burning. But there was nothing to be said. It was clear that his earlier commendation was now an international incident, and he was being made the scapegoat.

"What should I do now, sir?"

"Do? Go keep your appointment. But be prepared to do whatever they ask of you."

"Sir?" Schweiger found it hard to believe what he had just heard.

"You'll know what to do when the time comes." With that, the man stormed down the stairs, leaving Schweiger shaken on the landing.

What he was shortly to discover is that they wanted him to do the unthinkable—to willfully edit the entry in his official sea log regarding the sinking of the *Lusitania* by adding language indicating that after seeing the survivors in the water, he could not, in respect of humanity, fire another torpedo. Such sentiments were never part of an official log, which simply recorded events. Besides, the truth is that he did not launch a second strike because there was no need to waste a precious torpedo; the liner was doomed with one. But the revised version is the one that would be released to the public, pretending to be humane when no humanity had been shown.

* * *

"Tell me about the inquest."

"Are you sure you feel up to it?"

"I'm sure I feel like I've been in this uncomfortable bed for the greatest part of my life. I need something to distract me."

When Avery first awakened, he was deathly ill, as much a reaction to the ether as to the effects of the surgery. But as time passed, allowing the gas to dissolve within his system, his good spirits returned in surprisingly short time. When Bill expressed surprise at how quickly his strength seemed to return, he had replied, "Before I felt as if I was dying; now I know that I'm living."

"All right, I'll tell you about it. It was really quite compelling. John Horgan is the coroner of Cork County. He called the inquest as 'an inquiry into the cause of death for two males and three females whose corpses had been brought in on the rescue ship *Heron*.' Although they are just five out of what appears to be more than 1,200 passengers and crew who died, they are the ones that give him jurisdiction."

"More than 1,200? That's more than half of all the people on board."

"And the count is likely to climb. There are still bodies being washed up onshore nearly every day."

"Did you get to testify?"

"Nah. They didn't need me. The ship's bugler testified, since he was high up on the bridge when it happened, along with some passengers and crew. But what everyone was really there for was to hear Captain Turner."

"And how did the old man do for himself? I always had a sense he was somewhat above it all, maybe even out of touch."

"I don't know about that. To me his replies to the questions were honest and forthright, in spite of the overwhelming strain that he was under. He looked like a man twenty years older than he is—and he's pretty old to start with."

"What were the questions?"

"Things like, 'Did you know of the German warnings posted in the New York papers?' which was a stupid question. Of course he answered that he did. Then they asked him if the *Lusitania* was unarmed, and he said that it was absolutely unarmed, in spite of what some people sympathetic to the Germans have suggested. Then he told them about the steps he'd taken to protect people when we came into the war zone, like ordering the lifeboats to be swung out and watertight bulkhead doors to be closed. Things like that."

"But he didn't talk about keeping the ship under full speed, did he? Because he couldn't talk about that!"

"No, he couldn't say that. But he did answer all their questions about speed, including that we were going only eighteen knots when we were hit. That had to be embarrassing for him."

Avery shook his head. "We know all this stuff. Was there anything new?"

Bill pondered for a moment, trying to recall the testimony. He'd been so worried about Avery that it had been hard for him to concentrate. "There were two things that surprised me. The first was when a juror asked him if he'd ever wired ahead to the Admiralty to ask for protection."

"What was his answer to that, given that we were out there as naked as a jaybird?"

"He said that he had not and then added, 'I leave that to them. It is their business.'"

"That's just what you'd expect him to say, isn't it? They left us out there all alone, and he didn't take the trouble to ask about it. What else?"

"The coroner asked him if he'd received any special instructions, and he said he had but that he was not at liberty to say what they were. He told the jurors that he had followed those instructions."

"What do you suppose that was about? What kind of special instructions?"

Bill shrugged. "I don't know, but people outside the courtroom said they thought he received a directive to put into Queenstown, rather than going on to Liverpool. That would explain why we were so close to the headland, rather than farther out to sea as the Admiralty suggested."

"Probably one of those things we'll never know. You can be sure the Admiralty will do everything to cover its role in all this."

"That seems to be what's happening to Turner. The newspapers are reporting that 'anonymous sources in the Admiralty' are suggesting that he was either incompetent or in league with the Germans."

Avery nearly killed himself as he jerked up at that. "He is not in league with the Germans! That's preposterous. Why would someone allow himself to be put in danger by setting his own ship up to be torpedoed? That's ridiculous!"

"Calm down. I'm only telling you what I've heard. There are all kinds of rumors out there."

"Well, what else came out of the hearing?"

"Just more questions on what happened after the ship was struck. The captain alleged that everyone remained calm and that more lives would have been saved had he been able to slow the ship's forward progress. He blames the speed for the problems we had in lowering the lifeboats, as well as for the boats that became unusable on the port side because of the severe list."

"He's probably right in that, although from what I could see, people weren't remaining calm."

Bill laughed. "You think not? It was absolute pandemonium where I was. Perhaps they were all stiff and reserved up on the bridge, but out on the decks, people were screaming and shouting in an all-out panic."

Bill hesitated for a moment so that Avery could calm down. With his wound still open, he had to remain steady. "At any rate," he finally continued, "when it was all over, the coroner asked if the Germans had given any warning, to which Turner replied emphatically that they had not—just shot their torpedo and, as I remember him saying it, 'the whole lot went up in the air.' The coroner then looked around the room and told Turner that we all sympathized with him and that the *Lusitania* was the victim of a terrible crime. He commended him for his courage and recognized the deep feelings he must have."

"What did he do then?"

"That's the amazing thing—he started sobbing. Captain Turner just sat there and wept."

Avery took a deep breath. "Maybe he's not so bad. It was the Germans, after all, who did it. Those of us who work for Cunard were at the mercy of the Germans and the Admiralty."

Bill was a little amazed at how quickly people formed up alliances. Avery was not usually the type to take the side of officers, but when the reputation and good name of a ship was on the line, it was different.

"Well, the coroner declared that the full responsibility for the murder of all those people was on the officers of the submarine and even on the Kaiser himself."

"He said that?"

"He did." Bill smiled. "In fact, press reports have gone out to that effect all around the world—much to the chagrin of the Admiralty."

"What's the Admiralty got to say about that?" Avery was indignant again.

"Apparently the coroner received a telegram just an hour or two after the inquest was concluded instructing him not to take any independent action until officials from the Admiralty could arrive. I guess they want to control it all. At any rate, he just scoffed and said it was his right to hold a hearing and that the report had gone out anyway."

"Good for him." Avery raised an arm as a sign of triumph. But it was a mistake to do so, as evidenced by the involuntary yelp of pain that escaped.

Bill sat with him a few more minutes before saying, "I need to go for a bit. First, I need to get some money. Mum has said she'll wire some from our savings accounts."

"I certainly hope Cunard will pay for all this surgery," said Avery darkly.

"I believe they will. I just need to get an apartment that I can move you to in a few days. We can't leave the country until they sew up your side. Also, I need to get in touch with Mr. Stringham."

"I'm glad he's all right. You still need to tell me about your days in New York City."

Bill stood up and stretched. He'd spent most of the past four days here. "I will. Another time, though."

"Before you go . . ." said Avery tentatively.

"Yes?"

"Well, you've been great to be with me."

"You'd have done it for me."

"Right, but still." It was obvious he had something he wanted to say.

"Tell me . . ."

"I was just wondering if you'd maybe say a prayer. I know it's what Mum would like, and I think maybe I would too."

"A prayer?" Then Bill nodded. "I will. I have already. But it would be good to say it out loud like we did when we were all at home." He went over and closed the door, and then came back to the bed, where he knelt by Avery's side.

Chapter 23

His Majesty's Royal Navy

Liverpool, England

Bill's mother wiped her cheek as Bill gave her a hug. "It doesn't seem right, me and Avery going off with Brother Stringham like this and leaving you here by yourself. I'll miss you more than you can possibly know," she said.

Bill broke off the hug, held his mother by her shoulders, and smiled at her. "It'll be all right, Mum. I'll be off soon enough, anyway." He was so tired of all the emotions that had overwhelmed him in the last four months that he didn't see how he could stand anything else. About a week after the sinking, Ruth had accompanied Everett to Kinsale, where he rented a small apartment to continue his recovery while staying close to Bill and Avery. When she knew they would be all right, Ruth had made her way to Scotland and had already written them a long letter.

Six weeks after the sinking, Avery was well enough to travel, and the three of them had made their way to the Irish coast by train, where they caught a small transport ship back to Liverpool. Everett was well enough by that point to go on to London to conduct his business and now had returned. While recuperating in Ireland with Avery, he and the boys had spent many hours talking about America and about the opportunities there. It was during those conversations that the present plan had been developed. Now, after constant doting by both Clara Shafer and Mary Winnel, Avery was doing much better, even though he'd lost so much weight it was difficult for some of his friends to even recognize him. Worse, there was no sign that he was able to put any weight back on. It was clear he'd never be the same. Cunard had accepted responsibility and had agreed to a small pension to compensate him for his disability.

This disability was why the family had come to the decision they had—encouraged by Everett and, indirectly, his wife, Annie, in America. Clara had decided to immigrate to America, and Avery was going to accompany her. It would put her close to the Church, and they would see if it could open new doors for Avery. If all worked out well, he would send for Mary and Frankie, since they had decided to get married. If not, he would return to England to live with her there.

"I'm still not sure about this," said Avery to Bill. "You should be the one going to America to help find John Todd's sister. He was your friend, after all."

"I never thought of him as a friend. And yet, in the end, he saved my friend and treated me decently. Mr. Stringham is certain that Todd's remorse was genuine, and he has forgiven him. So I guess I have to as well. At any rate, it is important that you and Brother Stringham find his sister and tell her his story."

"Like I said, you're the one who should go. You know more about it than I do."

Bill shook his head. "No. I have to do my part for England by joining the navy. Meanwhile, you need to do what's right for you and Mary. Besides, someone needs to watch out for Mum."

Bill was to report to active duty at the Scapa Flow—home to the British Fleet in the islands off Northern Scotland. He didn't know yet what his assignment would be on board, but it didn't really matter. The one thing he had made clear to the enlisting officer was that he wanted to be on anti-submarine duty.

Avery took a couple of shallow breaths. "To tell the truth, I'm a little scared, Bill. The thought of picking up and starting all over—I just don't know."

"I know the Stringhams are happy to have you stay in their apartment in Salt Lake City for as long as you need. I've been with them enough to know that they're sincere about things like that. Once you're settled, you and Mum can get your own place, and then Mary and Frankie will come join you. And after the war, I'll come see you."

"But if you should stay and support England, why not me?"

Bill felt a bit of panic well up inside. In spite of the soundness of the plan, Avery kept wanting to back out. Now they were standing on the deck of a Cunard liner that was to take them to America, and he was having doubts yet again. Bill suspected it had a lot to do with Mary, who at this very moment was tearfully hugging Clara good-bye.

"The reason you should go is because here in England you'll always be on the disabled list. The doctor said that with all the internal injuries you suffered, in addition to your kidney, you'll never be able to do the kind of manual labor that is expected of folks like us. In America you can become a teacher or maybe even a professor."

"You keep saying that, but it makes no sense. I'm not from . . ."

"That's why I keep saying it. You want to judge things by what we know. But the Stringhams have made it abundantly clear that class doesn't matter there. For as smart and as well read as you are, you're certain to be accepted into the Brigham Young Academy. From there it's up to you what to do with your life. It will be on your own merit and abilities, not on chance of birth or anything or anyone else."

Avery shook his head. "It doesn't make sense to me, but what else can I do? I don't want to live my life being pitied."

"Give it a try. If it doesn't work, you can always come home."

Avery nodded. "Well, I guess I am up for a change of scenery, then. But I'll miss my little brother."

Bill smiled, even though his heart hurt at the thought of them leaving.

"You're not really a little brother anymore—you are a man and I am proud of you."

Bill gave Avery a gentle hug. Avery moved over to Mary to say his private good-bye. Little Frankie clung to him for dear life.

Bill turned to his mother. "I think you'll love living in America."

She reached over and took him into an embrace. "You're a fine son, Bill Shafer. A credit to us all." He allowed himself to enjoy the feeling of his mother's grasp. Even though she was a small woman, she was strong, and not just physically.

Finally, Bill turned to Everett Stringham. "I'm glad I found that Book of Mormon. Like you told me once, it has changed my life, but not in the way you expected. I still haven't even read it yet."

Everett smiled. "Perhaps you will while at sea. I'm going to miss you. I'll pray for you every day that you are safe through this war."

Bill returned his embrace. "Thank you for all you've done for me and my family. Please give my regards to Mrs. Stringham."

"I will."

Bill straightened up and stepped back from these people who meant so much to him. "Well, I have to get myself ready to serve in His Majesty's Navy."

They were startled by the blast of the great steam horn. "It's time for us to be off," Avery said.

Bill went over to Mary, put his arm through hers while taking Frankie by the hand, and with that they made their way to the gangplank and down to the pier. He was grateful that the international outrage against Germany had forced the Kaiser to withdraw their policy of unrestricted warfare at sea, so at least he didn't have to worry about this ship being sunk on the crossing.

Bill and Mary waved to the family as the ship pulled away from the pier and then watched until it disappeared from sight. Bill felt very alone. "Let me walk you home, Mary."

"No, you've got to go to the train station. I always made Avery late, and I don't want to do it to you."

"But . . ."

"But I know perfectly well how to find my way home." She smiled. "God answered my prayers, you know, by saving you and Avery. I have every confidence that He can help me make it to my flat."

Bill smiled. "He's a lucky man, my older brother."

The two hugged and Mary whispered, "Take care of yourself, Bill Shafer. You're part of our family now."

Bill decided he liked that.

He waited for a few moments as Mary and Frankie disappeared from sight. Somehow he knew it would work out for them and for Avery.

While walking toward the train station, he considered his resolve to serve king and country in this desperate fight. Bill Shafer was about to become the hunter, rather than the hunted. As the station came into view, he said as confidently as he could, "God save England!"

Author's Notes

There are many questions that can't be answered in a novel because the format simply doesn't lend itself to a thorough examination of all the historical detail. I've included a selected bibliography of some of the books, video, and websites I studied while preparing to write this story. The various technical references in the novel are accurate, to the best of my knowledge, and I included facts and figures only if they were corroborated by two or more sources. Still, this is a novel, and all the events surrounding the characters are fiction, (although plausible, based on the real-life experiences of those who survived the great disaster), and this story does not substitute for thorough historical research.

Because the story didn't lend itself to continuing the discussion of what happened after the sinking, here are some of the things I learned. I hope you find it interesting.

What caused the second explosion?

When I first read about the *Lusitania,* more than forty years ago, conventional wisdom held that the ship must have been carrying a secret payload of explosives, since nothing else could account for such massive destruction from the second explosion. This conclusion was supported by the German government's strong assertion that only one torpedo was fired. Now that the sunken wreck of the *Lusitania* has been found and thoroughly examined, it's been established that the *Lusitania* was *not* carrying contraband. Other theories were advanced, such as a coal dust or a boiler explosion. The most recent evidence is pretty clear that an explosion of the extremely high-pressure steam lines that passed between the boiler rooms and the steam turbines is the most likely explanation. That would account for the power of the blast as well as explaining why the pressure in the turbines dropped so precipitously, making the ship uncontrollable. Of all the theories offered, this is the one that makes the most sense to me.

What role did Captain Turner play in the disaster?

To his dying day, Captain Turner asserted that his decision to slow the ship and hold a steady course for a four-point bearing was the prudent thing to do. He's about the only one who felt that way.

In view of what we know today, it was an open invitation to destruction. But even so, Turner did not deserve the smear campaign the British Admiralty tried to foist on him. In fact, it was a scandal. First Sea Lord (the military head of the Royal Navy) said at the time, "The certainty is absolute that Captain Turner is not a fool, but a knave! It is my profound hope that Captain Turner will be arrested after the inquiry, whatever the outcome." In other words, he was asserting treason on the part of Turner and collaboration with the Germans to bring the ship into harm's way. As preposterous as that claim was, the Lord of the Admiralty, Winston Churchill (the political head of the Royal Navy), responded, "Fully concur! We shall pursue the Captain without check!"

Churchill is one of my personal heroes, but he was way out of line here. The likely explanation for their dirty campaign against Turner is that the failed Gallipoli campaign in the Mediterranean had turned into an unmitigated disaster for the navy, and the last thing the Admiralty needed was another scandal. So they tried to make it someone else's fault. But it was their problem, since they had taken responsibility for directing the course ships should follow when passing Ireland and coming into port. They should have communicated the dangers the *Lusitania* faced in much greater detail with specific instructions on how to proceed. For a ship so large and famous, they should also have sent a destroyer escort, but they did not. Some have suggested very dark motives to the Admiralty, alleging a conspiracy to leave the ship in harm's way on the assumption that an attack would provoke the United States into a more active role in the war. I hope that's not true, and nothing is on record to support it.

More likely, they simply neglected the great ocean liner, thus leaving the ship exposed to her terrible fate. In the official British inquiry, Lord Mersey showed himself to be a man of integrity when he exonerated Turner, placing the full blame on the Germans. Not only was this the humane thing to do, but it actually served British interests more fully than it would have to place the blame on negligence or incompetence.

What eventually became of Captain Turner?

In November 1915, Captain Turner was given command of a small freighter named the *Ultonia* and sailed from France to Quebec, Canada. In the fall of 1916, he was assigned to the *Ivernia,* which, almost unbelievably, was torpedoed and sunk off the coast of Greece. Once again Turner survived. That was his last command. For his long and illustrious career he was awarded the Order of the British Empire, but he was always remembered and often scorned for his role in the sinking of the *Lusitania*. Turner died in retirement in June 1933.

What happened to U-boat Captain Walther Schweiger?

Schweiger was killed in action when *U-88* hit a British mine, sinking on September 5, 1917. He sunk forty-nine surface ships in his short but successful naval career.

Did the sinking of the* Lusitania *bring America into the war?

For some reason, most people today believe that this was the direct cause of our entry into the war. But it clearly was not, since America didn't declare war for more than a year and a half after the sinking—not that the American public wasn't stirred up by the sinking, with many calling for a declaration of war. But President Woodrow Wilson was still a pacifist at this point, and he declared self-righteously, "There is such a thing as a man being too proud to fight. There is such a thing as a nation being so right that it does not need to convince others by force that it is right." But Wilson did lodge formal protests against Germany, demanding an apology, reparations to the families of the victims, and a promise not to sink neutral ships. Eventually the Kaiser was forced to give in to these demands, which postponed war for America until the next time Germany declared unrestricted submarine warfare.

The direct cause of our entry into World War I was the Zimmerman Telegram in which the German Foreign Secretary, Arthur Zimmerman, sent a coded message to Germany's ambassador in the United States, encouraging him to entice Mexico to launch a war against the United States, offering to return the states of Texas, Arizona, and New Mexico as a reward. The Mexican government ignored the offer, but when the British released the intercepted telegram to the press, the American public outrage was so overwhelming that Wilson was forced to go to war. Germany was prepared for that, hoping they could finish off France and England before America could mobilize and make any real difference in the war. That belief was a fatal mistake for Germany.

Did Germany have a side in this story?

Hopefully I already communicated the outrage that Germans felt at America's support of the British naval blockade of Germany, while actively trading with England. The effect was to starve German civilians while feeding the British. This did not, in my opinion, justify the sinking of the *Lusitania,* but it does provide context for why the German government felt justified in doing so—particularly since they published their formal warning prior to the ship's departure from New York City.

Has the wreck of the* Lusitania *been found?

In her marvelous book, *Lusitania—An Epic Tragedy,* author Diana Preston summarizes the various expeditions to find the ship on pages 371–75. To summarize her account, the ship was found by a salvage consortium in 1935. After a single confirming dive by a professional diver, the group was driven off by bad weather. No one visited the wreck again until 1960, when an American explorer, John Light, made forty-two dives on behalf of British and American television. The water was cold and murky, so photographs were inconclusive. Further dives were made in 1982 and again by Bob Ballard (the man who found the *Titanic*) in 1993 using remotely operated vehicles equipped with modern video and lighting. Since then, there have been multiple dives, with much clearer photos. Men have actually walked through the superstructure. Fortunately, the Irish Arts Ministry placed an

International Heritage Protection Order on the wreck and its contents to prevent wholesale destruction of the wrecked vessel. Now all dives must be authorized in advance, and anything to be removed from the site must be approved and cataloged.

I hope you enjoyed the story. Please feel free to visit me at www.jerryborrowman.com, where you can submit questions or comments as well as look at the other books I've written or coauthored. Thanks for reading my books.

Selected Bibliography

Lusitania—An Epic Tragedy. Diana Preston. Berkley Publishing Group: New York. 2002.

The Last Voyage of the Lusitania. A. A. Hoehling and Mary Hoehling. Madison Books: Lanham, Maryland. 1996.

Sinking of the Lusitania—Terror at Sea. DVD. Discovery Channel. Distributed by Image Entertainment: Chatsworth, California. 2008.

The Lusitania: The Life, Loss, and Legacy of an Ocean Legend. Daniel Allen Butler. Stackpole Books, Mechanicsburg, Pennsylvania. 2000.

The Age of Cunard. Daniel Allen Butler. Lighthouse Press: Annapolis, Maryland. 2003.

RMS Lusitania. www.wikipedia.com. Accessed in 2010.

Lusitania Online—The Home Port for RMS Lusitania. www.lusitania.net. Accessed in 2010.